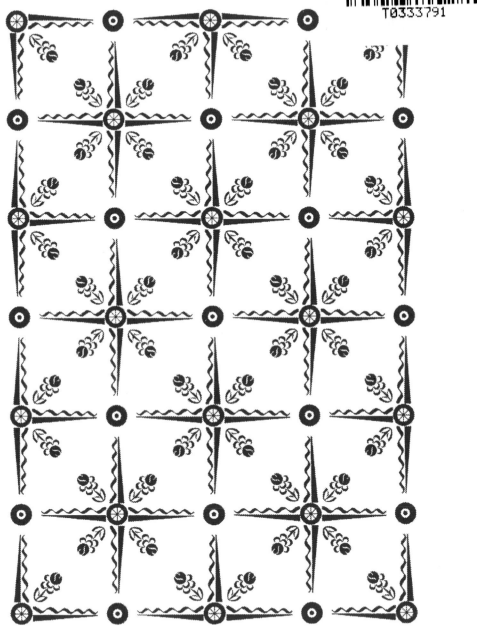

BERTHOLD WOLPE

A
RETROSPECTIVE
SURVEY

BERTHOLD WOLPE AT FABER & FABER

Berthold Wolpe joined Faber & Faber in 1941, at the end of one of the firm's most brilliant decades, during which the format and house style of the Faber book had been established by Richard de la Mare. Many artists had designed jackets for de la Mare – Barnett Freedman, Rex Whistler, Edward Bawden, McKnight Kauffer, Paul Nash, Eric Fraser, Reynolds Stone, Herbert Bayer and Moholy-Nagy – and Berthold must have found the creative atmosphere in the production department very congenial when he arrived. With the outbreak of war, economy of means had become necessary and Berthold immediately showed that calligraphy and typography by themselves could replace the elaborate art- and process- work the firm had experimented with in the thirties. The distinctiveness of a Wolpe jacket – which he always insisted was a small poster for the book – was the idiosyncratic and highly expressive lettering or type display of title and author, printed on stock paper. No-one else at the time quite matched his ingenuity and originality in doing this, and his binding brasses for the spines of books became an unmistakable Wolpe hallmark.

He was a master of display typography and showed incidentally how only the designer of a face can fully understand its potential. *Albertus* in its creator's hands – in all sizes and weights – has never been seen in more permutations than in the thousands of Wolpe's jacket fronts for the Faber list over forty years. But he also had a subtle appreciation of the character of classic faces such as *Caslon*, *Baskerville* and *Bell*, and one of his most handsome formal jackets was for *A History of the Old English Letter Foundries*, which he was instrumental in having reissued.

Some of his most resourceful and effective devices appeared on utilitarian wartime books and pamphlets about compost, gardening, first-aid, self-defence and cookery, as well as the literary and intellectual writings on the main Faber list. For many people the *Albertus* fount became identified with the Faber imprint and Wolpe showed that he could handle asymmetry as well as centred layouts effortlessly. De la Mare, for whom he was working, recognised his great gifts, and although a most self-effacing person in his own visual tastes, allowed Berthold to initial his drawn jacket designs W or BLW.

His colleagues soon realised they had a formidable scholar and collector, as well as an expressive genius, in their midst, and in the sixties and seventies his own writings and research resulted in a number of important works on type and design, calligraphy, handwriting, and other related matters. His bohemian appearance, his wit and his extrovert personality became part of the culture of Faber & Faber, and he formed a remarkable partnership with David Bland, a fine scholar and designer of a very different kind, who returned to run the production department after his experience as a prisoner of war.

The significance of Wolpe as a designer and type master was not of course confined to 24 Russell Square. His visual language became widely recognised in the graphic world, especially among young designers and connoisseurs, and is now part of the history of British publishing up to the computer revolution – a development that Wolpe would certainly have known how to exploit. Much of his repertoire as a designer, a teacher and historian was drawn from his prodigious accumulation of rare books and ephemera, which filled his home and his rooms at Fabers. When his office was cleared on his retirement a huge hoard of *disjecta membra* was uncovered among the precious books and papers, including a full-size Union Jack with flagpole, which he had retrieved from a builder's skip on a lunchtime ramble in Bloomsbury. Nothing was beyond the range of his magpie curiosity. All this extraordinary material is now a major visual resource. It has become a collection of national importance in its own right, destined, one hopes, for the Type Museum in London, in Wolpe's *Centenary Year, 2005*.

John Bodley, 1930 – 2004

Faber 75th Anniversary, September 2004

PHOTO: GEOFFREY IRELAND

BERTHOLD WOLPE

A RETROSPECTIVE SURVEY

THE MERRION PRESS

LONDON 2005

First published by the V&A and Faber & Faber
in 1980 as a catalogue for the V&A retrospective
exhibition of the work of Berthold Wolpe

copyright © Berthold Wolpe 1980

Second edition published in 2005 by
the Merrion Press, 100 Hackford Road,
London SW9 0QU, as a prelude to the
Berthold Wolpe Centenary in 2005

Printed and bound in 2005 and donated to
the *Centenary* by Ken Smith at Smith Settle,
Printers & Binders, Ilkley Road, Otley,
West Yorkshire LS21 3JP

New text, cover design and illustration
copyright © Merrion Press 2005

Faber ISBN 0 571 22728 7

First edition written and designed by Berthold
Wolpe and printed at the Westerham Press by
Rowley Atterbury: film-set in *Pegasus* using
first-time fonts especially prepared by Matthew
Carter for Mergenthaler Linotype, after the
design of Berthold Wolpe. *Pegasus* was first cut
in 16 point at Monotype in 1938

New material set in *Trajanus* [Stempel 1939]
designed by Warren Chappell: fellow-pupil
with Berthold Wolpe and Fritz Kredel,
at the Rudolf Koch workshop in Offenbach

Cover design by Phil Cleaver & Sue Shaw,
set in Wolpe's *Albertus* [Monotype 1934];
Berthold Wolpe *portrait* by Charles Mozley
for the Frankfurt Book Fair Catalogue,
printed by Rowley Atterbury in 1956

Flyleaf: see catalogue entry 58

*The Merrion Press is grateful to the
V&A and Faber & Faber for their
kind permission to reissue this book
and to all those generously concerned
with its design, printing and production*

BLW 1905–1989

CONTENTS

Colour plates A, B, C, D following item 13
and E, F, G, H following item 133

PREFACE AND
ACKNOWLEDGEMENTS

This exhibition at the Victoria and Albert Museum coincides with the 75th birthday of Dr Berthold Wolpe RDI.

His oeuvre is important and diverse. The exhibition is designed to represent as fully as possible the scope and variety of his work. It includes tapestries, metal artifacts and jewellery, made by the designer himself which gives the display a somewhat broader dimension than that usually to be found in Library exhibitions.

It also shows how he excels both as a designer of widely used and distinguished typefaces, such as Pegasus, Hyperion and Albertus and as a book designer and illustrator of note.

His skill as a teacher is displayed in the teaching alphabets, which cover the main styles of lettering of the Western World. Other exhibits show him in the role of author, researcher and editor.

The vein of good humour which can be glimpsed in much of his work explains in part the enthusiasm with which his many friends and colleagues have greeted and supported this event.

Preparation of this exhibition was initiated by Robert Kenedy, of the Library staff. His sudden and untimely death earlier this year has robbed the Museum of a colleague who is sadly missed and who did much to make the exhibition possible.

The Museum would like to thank Robert Harling of House and Gardens for suggesting the exhibition in the first place.

We should like to express our thanks to the following for loans to the exhibition:

The Royal Mint; Christian Scheffler and the Klingspor Museum, Offenbach; Faber & Faber Ltd; London Transport; Banco Espagnol, London; Mrs H. Jacobi; the executors of the late Theodore Besterman; Alex Gumb; The Merrion Press; Berthold Wolpe.

Gratitude is due for generous practical and financial help to:

J. G. Mercer of Redwood Burn Ltd; L. Edward Bentall of Bentalls Ltd; Des Edmonds of Conway Group Graphics Ltd; T. Wilkinson of the Folio Society Ltd; Mrs S. Keshavjee of Sainsbury's Ltd; Colin Brignall of Messrs Letraset Ltd; J. B. Latham of Monotype International and Michael Chater of Grosvenor Chater.

In this context we particularly wish to thank John Dreyfus; Rosemary Goad and John Bodley of Faber & Faber, and W. Kilian, Cultural Attaché, Embassy of the Federal Republic of Germany.

Essential work on producing this survey was done by the following: Sue Fowler, who assisted in designing the exhibition, prepared the bibliography; Helen Dore the index; A. S. Osley and Anthony Kitzinger gave editorial advice and help over the text; Des Edmonds of Conways made the Pegasus founts; and John Parfitt and Jim Hollamby of Westerham Press produced the book.

Last, but not least, we wish to thank our colleagues in the Library, who have helped with the preparation of this exhibition including Miss B. Cole for clerical assistance; also P. Spruyt de Bay and C. N. R. Nichols of the Museum Photographic Studio, and N. Bird, Publications Officer for unfailing interest and advice.

Peter Castle, 1980

INTRODUCTION

Berthold Wolpe is seventy-five years old, and the retrospective exhibition of his work commemorates this event.

He was born at Offenbach near Frankfurt. Instead of entering a university he chose to become an apprentice with a firm of metalworkers. Here he learned gold, silver and copper smithing, chasing and engraving. This basic training in metal, combined with a nascent passion for calligraphy and inscriptional lettering, led almost inevitably to an interest in type design. He became a pupil of Rudolf Koch at the Offenbach Kungstgewerbeschule from 1924 to 1928. His early work naturally shows Koch's influence. Today Wolpe still acknowledges his early debt to Koch; he states that, even if his own style has developed away from the Koch tradition, the directions in which it has moved would have obtained the approval of his old master.

From 1929 to 1933 he taught at the Frankfurt and Offenbach School of Art. During this period he designed his Hyperion type, which was commercially issued by the Bauer foundry, numerous ornaments and devices, and his copybook (Schriftvorlagen) intended, like the early Italian writing-books for the use of 'scribes, painters, sculptors, goldsmiths, embroiderers and other craftsmen'.

The critical point in his life was no doubt the decision in 1935 to leave Nazi Germany and to settle in England. The result is that the last forty-five years of his working life have been spent almost entirely in the country of his adoption.

In this short note one can mention only a few highlights of Wolpe's many-sided activities. While on a visit to England in 1932, he met Stanley Morison, who had been impressed by some lettering in bronze done by Wolpe and he invited the young German designer to come up with a type-face, for the Monotype Corporation, based on these bronze letters. The result was 'Albertus' (titling capitals in 1935; lower case in 1937; and bold and light versions in 1940). The new face had an immense success when first shown and it has become phenomenally successful during the last decade. 'Albertus' is strong, distinctive and economical. It successfully combines Gothic gravity and the classic Italian forms in an entirely contemporary way. Less well known, but a worthy partner, is his 'Pegasus' typeface.

After four years at the Fanfare Press with Ernest Ingham, Berthold Wolpe joined Faber & Faber where he worked with Richard de la Mare and David Bland. He remained with the firm until retirement from full-time employment in 1975. Wolpe has designed at least 1500 jackets, probably hundreds more, for Faber books. As a result of a variety of techniques, but especially of freely drawn lettering, his jackets often echo the atmosphere of the books' contents in an uncanny way. When he designs the book itself, his patience and skill are infinite. I well remember seeing him paste up with his own hands my book on Mercator – which is certainly a very fine example of the typographer's art.

His ideas for book design are nourished by a wealth of historical knowledge. He has not only played a full part in the activities of the Printing Historical Society and the Double Crown Club but has also undertaken many pieces of serious research. He has, for example, written on Jean de Beauchesne,[1] Caslon,[2] Figgins,[3] and alphabets in medieval manuscripts.[4] He has also edited an Elizabethan handwriting manual which he discovered in the Bodleian Library,[5] and Steingruber's ARCHITECTURAL ALPHABET, Merrion Press, 1973. His collaboration with Alfred Fairbank has been of great importance because it resulted, among other things, in RENAISSANCE HANDWRITING (1959), an essential book for the serious student of this subject.

Berthold Wolpe has always attached much importance to his work as a teacher. For some years he taught at the Camberwell School of Art; after that he was tutor (and later visiting lecturer) at the School of Graphic Design in the Royal College of Art. At present he teaches lettering at the City & Guilds of London School of Art. His Edith Burnett Memorial Lecture, delivered at the British Academy where he showed several specimens of students' work, aroused a good deal of interest.

It would have been surprising if the talents of a man who has accomplished so much so well had not been formally recognized in some way. He was made a Royal Designer for Industry in 1959 and he was awarded an honorary doctorate by the Royal College of Art in 1968.

The following is an extract from the orator's citation when this degree was conferred:

'The right answer to the famous question "Où est la plume de ma tante?", if asked by no matter who, of any age or clime, would most probably be: "in the collection of Berthold Wolpe". For besides being a renowned calligrapher, designer of typefaces and of books, bibliophile and craftsman in precious metals, Mr Wolpe is one of the greatest magpie-historians of our age; he is consumed by an unquenchable curiosity concerning "all trades, their gear and tackle and trim. All things counter, original, spare and strange" as Gerald Manley Hopkins wrote; and especially all implements concerned with the making of letter-forms, whether by pen, incision or printing process. For eight years, this College was enriched by his presence as teacher of his variegated lore, and many persons here present will recall nostalgically the shy but irresistible enthusiasm with which he was wont to pull out from specially designed recesses deep in his gamekeeperish garb, as it might be a pair of Byzantine scissors or a Hispano-Moorish inkhorn. . . .'

After a lifetime's obsession with the alphabet in all its manifestations, Wolpe believes that the letter forms of the past have a lot to tell us today. Yet he deprecates painstaking imitation as an end in itself. He considers that the traditional should be adapted, where

[1] Journal of the Society for Italic Handwriting, No. 82; SCRIBES AND SOURCES, 1980
[2] 'Caslon Architectural', ALPHABET 1964
[3] VINCENT FIGGINS TYPE SPECIMENS 1801 AND 1815, PHS 1967
[4] 'Florilegium Alphabeticum', CALLIGRAPHY & PALAEOGRAPHY, 1965
[5] A NEWE BOOKE OF COPIES 1574

necessary, to modern needs and techniques. Thus, when he uses Italic on his book jackets, the letters, almost always hand drawn (unlike the Letraset compositions of other designers) are not copybook versions. They are the formal Italic that the classic Italian writing-master Arrighi Vicentino might have evolved, had he been working today. Similarly, his type-designs, and for that matter his informal handwriting, are rooted in traditional soil but flower in a manner that is clearly of the 20th century.

He has been elected to the James P. R. Lyell Readership in Bibliography for the year 1981–2 and this will entail his giving six lectures at Oxford on some aspects of calligraphy and picture printing.

A. S. Osley, 1980

from an article in the Journal of the Society for Italic Handwriting, No.87, Summer 1976

Tapestries, Metalwork, Jewellery and Coins

1

TWO PASSOVER TAPESTRIES

made in Rudolf Koch's workshop in 1927 after designs of Berthold Wolpe and embroidered on linen by Stefanie Freise, Anni Kredel and Hertha Jobst for Dr Siegfried Guggenheim

a. Fourteen lines of the German text of Psalm 114 in uncials, alternating with the opening lines of Psalm 118 in Hebrew with decorated motifs. Brown, blue, black and red.

b. Thirty further lines of Psalm 118, verses 5–18 also in uncials; at the base three words in Hebrew: Passover, unleavened bread and bitter herbs. Ochre, blue, black and red.

Lent by the Klingspor Museum, Offenbach am Main
240 × 130 cm

2

TAPESTRY

designed by Berthold Wolpe in 1930 and embroidered on linen in Rudolf Koch's workshop

Psalm text

WEISE MIR, HERR, DEINEN WEG

Eight lines of capital letters, outlined in blue with red centre line, within red and red-and-green bars. Between the lines of lettering are seven bands of linear abstract designs in black.

See plate A
220 × 120 cm

3

FRANKFURT TAPESTRY

designed by Berthold Wolpe in 1932 and woven by Ursula Koch the next year in the tapestry workshop of Rudolf Koch

Koch had received some red and white silks and suggested that they be used for a wall hanging with the arms of the town of Frankfurt as the subject. Koch and his two assistants, Fritz Kredel and Wolpe, tried their hand at the Frankfurt arms: a white eagle on a red ground (argent on gules).

Koch and Kredel's solutions to the problem were strictly heraldic. Wolpe however incorporated the eagle into a composition that included the cathedral tower, the town hall, and the old bridge and river – all characteristic landmarks of the town. The text is from a poem by Hölderlin.

See plate B
147 × 93 cm

4

COPPER VESSEL

raised from a flat sheet of copper and incised with the inscription: SOLI DEO GLORIA in capital letters. 1925

See plate C
height 14 cm
diameter 21 cm

5

COPPER VESSEL

Bowl of truncated cone shape
raised from a flat sheet of heavy copper, on
a tripod base made of yellow bronze. 1926

height 14 cm
diameter 28 cm

6

COPPER VESSEL

Bowl, raised from a flat sheet of heavy copper
over a four-shafted base in brass. 1926

height 14 cm
diameter 28 cm

7

COPPER EWER AND BASIN

designed and made by Berthold Wolpe
in 1926

Incised on the rim of the basin an inscription in
Hebrew of the benediction for the washing of
hands.

Formerly in the collection of Dr Siegfried
Guggenheim. Lent by the Klingspor Museum,
Offenbach am Main   height of ewer c.40 cm
diameter of basin c.52 cm

8

WALL FOUNTAIN

A water container in copper with brass tap
and a basin also in copper, designed and
made by Berthold Wolpe in 1927

Acquired by the former Gewerbe Museum in
Darmstadt. Present whereabouts unknown. A
photograph is however reproduced in a special
issue of Philobiblon 1934, edited by Georg
Haupt and devoted to the work of Rudolf Koch
and his circle.

9

CANDELABRUM

This three-branched pricket candle-holder was
designed and made in brass, c.1927

Leg, stem and branch were cast as one unit. Two
of these units were bonded together with rivets
with a centre unit between.   height 43 cm
max. width 31 cm

10

SILVER BOWL

designed and made by Berthold Wolpe in
1927 for his mother Agathe Wolpe

height 5.4 cm
diameter 26 cm

11

SILVER BOWL

designed and made by Berthold Wolpe

19 BW 29 engraved on base

Lent by Mrs H. Jacobi

See plate D   height 4.9 cm
diameter 19.7 cm

12

SILVER FLAGON

designed by Berthold Wolpe c.1930
and made by Edward Fischer

On lid: SOLI DEO GLORIA engraved by the
designer.   height 33.3 cm

13

PENDANTS

a. Silver with an ivory dome set in gold over
a black onyx disc. 1928   3.9 cm
b. Silver with ivory hemisphere set in gold
within seven concentric rings. 1929   4.2 cm
See plate D

A

B

C

D

14

BROOCHES
designed and made by Berthold Wolpe
in 1928/9
a. Silver with black onyx   1.2 × 5.3 cm
b. Silver with lapis lazuli and coral 2.9 × 5.8 cm
c. Silver with agate disc   1.8 × 4.8 cm
See plate D

15

CIRCULAR PLAQUE
in cloisonné enamel
designed and made by Berthold Wolpe
in 1927
Text: SOLI DEO GLORIA in capital letters.
Colours: dark and light blue, red and white.
See plate C   diameter 10 cm

16

SQUARE TABLET
in champlevé enamel
designed and made by Berthold Wolpe in 1928
Text: SOLI DEO GLORIA with alpha and omega.
Colours: blue, green and red on copper gilt. See
plate C.

Also a blind impression on paper of the die
used to shape the thin piece of metal to receive
the enamel.   both 7.4 × 7.4 cm

17

PATTERNS AND ORNAMENTAL DESIGNS
Proof prints from metal plates designed,
chased and cut by Berthold Wolpe c.1933
Commissioned by Rudolf Koch, who intended
to produce them eventually in book form.
      c.17 × 18 cm

18

BRONZE MEDAL
showing a seven-branched candelabrum in
the centre of a tabernacle
Inscription reads: DU BIST MEINES FUSSES
LEUCHTE UND EIN LICHT AUF MEINEM
WEGE
On reverse incised a chasing hammer and the
date 1927.
Wolpe's journeyman examination piece, designed and made at the end of his apprenticeship as
a metal chaser.   7.1 cm

19

ROYAL MINT LONDON
According to the annual report (April 1961) of
the Deputy Master and Comptroller of the
Royal Mint: '... the opportunity was taken to
introduce a form of lettering (Albertus) and
beaded decorations different from those which
appear on other coins of The Queen's reign.'
a. Crown piece (five shillings), 1960
b. Crown piece (Churchill Memorial), 1965
Albertus was also used on other coins struck
at the Mint, e.g.: Jersey Penny, commemorative
issue, 1960 and on the coinage of Jamaica.

Other uses of Albertus are to be found on
decorations and medals, made at the Royal
Mint, e.g.: Ffennell Competition Medal;
College of Air Training Medal and the Bahamas
Badge of Honour.

Lent by the Royal Mint.

20

SPANISH MINT MADRID
For some years Albertus has been used as lettering style for all Spanish coins:
a. 1 peseta, 1975   c. 25 pesetas, 1975
b. 5 pesetas, 1975   d. 50 pesetas, 1975
Made available by Banco Espagnol, London.

HERE LIE THE ASHES OF THE POET
WALTER DE LA MARE, O.M.,C.H.
25 APRIL 1873 - 22 JUNE 1956
Onetime choir-boy of ST. PAUL'S

℄ Where blooms the flower when her petals fade,
Where sleepeth echo by earth's music made,
Where all things transient to the changeless win,
There waits the peace thy spirit dwelleth in.

Inscriptions and Lettering

21

BRONZE TABLET
in memory of Maria and Phillip Hahn
Rubbing of an inscription in bronze designed
and made by Berthold Wolpe in 1927

The letters are made by cutting back the ground
around them. This is the kind of inscription
Stanley Morison had seen reproduced in an
article by Rudolf Conrad in Gebrauchsgraphik,
Vol.4, No.8, 1927. Morison liked the quality of
the cut characters and in 1932 he asked Wolpe
to design a printing type in this style.

54×78.5 cm

22

BRONZE TABLET
in memory of Hans and Roland
von Ruckteschell

Photograph of inscription
designed and cut by Berthold Wolpe
in 1929.

67×46 cm

23

BRONZE TABLET
in memory of Maier Lindheimer
Model in plaster
designed and cut by Berthold Wolpe
in 1928.

40×35 cm

24

TOMBSTONE
in memory of Richard Freise

Photographs and rubbings of
monument in limestone
designed by Berthold Wolpe in 1930.

170×45 cm

25

STONE INSCRIPTION
in memory of Walter de la Mare (1873–1956)

Rubbing of an inscription on Welsh slate in the
crypt of St Paul's Cathedral, London.

Designed by Berthold Wolpe and cut by John
Andrews.   60.5×88 cm

26

ARCHITECTURAL LETTERING
Jewish Cemetery, Frankfurt am Main
The inscriptions were executed after the
designs of Berthold Wolpe in 1929

Three photographs showing:
a. Three-dimensional Hebrew letters forming
the inscription on the brickwork above the
entrance gates.
b. Bronze doors with embossed inscription in
Hebrew and German.
c. Detail of two long inscriptions in copper on
the architraves of the arcades around the court-
yard. Three-dimensional roman capital letters
with the unexpected use of a rounded E.

27

INSCRIPTION
Wilhelm Löhe
'Was will ich? Dienen will ich …'

Written in black-letter c.1930, when Berthold
Wolpe worked in the Offenbach Werkstatt. An
edition of this text was printed for a nursing
order and was given to members on enrolment.
Proof print from line-block.   44×28 cm

GOTTES
IST DER
ORIENT

GOTTES
IST DER
OCCIDENT

NORD
UND
SÜDLICHES
GELÄNDE

RUHT
IM FRIEDEN
SEINER
HÄNDE

28
INSCRIPTION
Psalm text
'Dein Wort ist meines Fusses Leuchte,
und ein Licht auf meinem Wege.'
Inscription in landscape format, versals with
thin serifs written in indian ink with a broad
pen, c.1930. 80×59 cm

29
COMPASS ROSE
This design by Berthold Wolpe is a part of a
large pictorial map of Germany made by Rudolf
Koch and Fritz Kredel with the collaboration of
Richard Bender and B.W. between 1925 and
1933. The design of the compass rose includes a
quatrain from Goethe's Westöstlicher Divan.
The map was first published by the Insel-Verlag,
Leipzig in 1934. size of rose 21×21 cm

30

INSCRIPTION
Johann Wolfgang von Goethe
'Und wenn mich am Tag die Ferne
Blauer Berge sehnlich zieht ...'

Poem of eight lines, written quickly with a broad pen in a nearly upright italic. Indian ink on cream paper. 1930
Reproduced in Lettering of To-day, published by The Studio Ltd, 1937.   66.5×44.5 cm

31

INSCRIPTION
Johann Wolfgang von Goethe
'Fetter Grüne, du Laub,
Am Rebengeländer ...'

Written in eight lines with a broad pen, with speed in a free cursive hand. Indian ink on unruled white paper.   52×40 cm

32

INSCRIPTION
Friedrich Hölderlin
'Mit gelben Blumen hängt
und voll mit wilden Rosen ...'

Poem of fourteen lines, written in a formal black-letter. Indian ink on red-painted paper.
1931   65×47 cm

33

INSCRIPTION
William Shakespeare; Sonnet LXV
'Since brass, nor stone, nor earth ...'

Written in indian ink in black-letter, 1931
Note on back: Berthold Wolpe, Lehrer an der Kunstschule, Frankfurt am Main.   64×50 cm

34

SIEGFRIED GUGGENHEIM
Offenbacher Haggadah
Offenbach am Main, Guggenheim, 1927
Several close friends of the author and publisher were responsible for producing this book. Rudolf Koch's Jessen type was used for setting the German text. Fritz Kredel provided the woodcut illustrations and Berthold Wolpe the lettering for some of the passages in Hebrew.
31×23.5 cm

THESE, IN THE DAY WHEN
HEAVEN WAS FALLING,
THE HOUR WHEN EARTHS
FOUNDATIONS FLED,
FOLLOWED THEIR MER=
CENARY CALLING AND
TOOK THEIR WAGES AND
ARE DEAD ·
epitaph on an army of Mercenaries

THEIR SHOULDERS HELD
THE SKY SUSPENDED · THEY
STOOD, AND EARTH'S
FOUNDATIONS STAY,
WHAT GOD ABANDONED
THESE DEFENDED,
AND SAVED THE SUM OF
THINGS FOR PAY ·
Æ Housman

35

INSCRIPTION
A. E. Housman

Epitaph for an Army of Mercenaries

Written by Berthold Wolpe in 1932 with a broad pen in indian ink, title and author's name in red.

Reproduced in catalogue of 'The Art of Letter', Scottish National Gallery of Modern Art, Edinburgh, 1970   67 × 50 cm

36

RUDOLF KOCH
and FRITZ KREDEL
Das Blumenbuch

a. Title-page design

In 1930 Rudolf Koch asked Wolpe for a title-page design for a special edition of twenty copies of this book which was composed of carefully rubbed proof prints from the wood-blocks on Japanese paper. Wolpe wrote a title page immediately, without ruling the paper. He intended to write it again more formally. Koch, however, liked the spontaneity and freedom of the rough and had Fritz Kredel cut it on wood.   30 × 21 cm

b. An intermediate wood engraver's proof of the first five lines of the title page.

37

DATE LETTER ALPHABET
Original drawing of 25 italic characters for hall-marking submitted to the Birmingham Assay Office c.1950   10 × 16 cm

38

HOMAGE TO HOLLAR
Sometime in 1977 a small group of people including the Czech cultural attaché gathered in the churchyard of St Margaret's, Westminster, where Wenceslaus Hollar (1607–77) is buried, to commemorate the tri-centenary of his death. Wolpe was asked to provide an inscription that could be fixed to the outside of the church for the ceremony. Flowers were deposited below this panel and it remained there in the open for a fortnight.   61 × 50.5 cm

39

TEACHING ALPHABETS
These poster-size sheets were all written freely and quickly in indian ink or black paint – often on unruled paper – with broad pen or flat brush, in the presence of the students at the Royal College of Art and at the City & Guilds of London Art School, to demonstrate lettering style and technique. Afterwards they were fixed to the wall to be used as exemplars for further study and for copying.

a. Roman square capitals on buff paper
                    52 × 72 cm
b. Uncial letters on one inch graph paper
                    38 × 51 cm
c. Black letter or textura minuscules on green paper   46 × 58 cm
d. Round gothic or rotunda on white paper
                    45 × 59.5 cm
e. Roman capitals and minuscules on yellow paper   77.5 × 49 cm
f. Italic minuscules on white paper   39 × 52 cm
g. Block or sanserif capitals on squared paper
                    41 × 54 cm

VERITAS

SCS ALBERTVS MAGNVS
SANCTITATE & DOCTRINA
CELEBER
QVEM PIVS PAPA XI
DOCTOREM VNIVERSALIS
ECCLESIAE DECLARAVIT
IPSE PRO NOBIS ORAT

ABCDEFGHIJKLMNOPQ
RSTUVWXYZ&MT

THIS FIRST SPECIMEN OF THE ALBERTUS CAPITALS DESIGNED BY BERTHOLD WOLPE IS PRESENTED
TO THE ALBERTVS MAGNVS AKADEMIE COLOGNE
BY THE ENGRAVERS THE MONOTYPE CORPORATION LIMITED AT 43 FETTER LANE IN LONDON
1937

Type-design:
Albertus, Hyperion, Tempest, Fanfare Ornaments, Pegasus, Sachsenwald, Decorata, and LTB Italic

ALBERTUS

When I first came to London in the summer of 1932, I met Mr Stanley Morison. He had seen photographs of some bronze inscriptions of mine which interested him and asked me to design for the Monotype Corporation a printing type of capital letters based on the lettering developed for these bronze inscriptions.

I had been through a fairly thorough training in a bronze foundry and in addition had done gold and silversmith work. Apart from this I was a student with Rudolf Koch and later became his assistant. Rudolf Koch, by the way, had a similar training and it was on his advice that I was apprenticed to the foundry. I owe Rudolf Koch, who died in April of 1934, more than I can say.

On the bronze inscriptions mentioned, the letters were not incised but raised; in other words the background was lowered and the outline only of the letters cut in. Such a metal inscription is cut with a chisel and not drawn with a pen, which gives it sharpness without spikiness, and as the outlines of the letters are cut from outside (and not from the inside outwards), this makes for bold simplicity and reduces the serifs to a bare minimum.

If you were to ink the inscription you could actually take an impression from it which, of course, would reverse the letters in mirror fashion. This sounds fairly easy to convert into a type, but when it came to preparing the working drawings for the cutting of the type careful adjustments had to be made to allow for a smooth working of all the innumerable combinations necessary in a printing type. The discipline involved in making an inscription is considerably less than that required for designing a printing type. But the experience gained in the one was of great help in the other. For instance, I found it justifiable to keep certain letters narrow, such as E, F, L, T, which are often used, as the visual effect is broadened by their horizontal lines. The advantage is especially obvious when these letters are doubled.

A lot of nonsense has been talked about the fact that a printing type has to be designed in a much larger size. In my opinion it should be designed as near as possible to its actual size and then the necessary optical adjustments have to be made for the various other sizes which make up the family. In the case of *Albertus* there was very little difference between the 72 pt and the bronze inscriptions which set the style.

This first size was cut in 1934 and shown for the first time as a new titling on the cover of the Monotype Recorder Book Number in the summer of 1935.

from Print in Britain, Vol.I, No.2, June 1953   BERTHOLD WOLPE

40

NAMING ALBERTUS
An early trial proof of Wolpe Titling 72pt
Monotype Series 324
dated 13 February 1935
At about this time the name Albertus was suggested by the designer to Stanley Morison. This exhibit shows the alteration to the name in Morison's hand. 25×20 cm

41

ALBERTUS ARRIVES
Monotype Recorder, London
Volume 34, No.2, Summer 1935
Albertus Titling 72pt appears for the first time on the front cover of this issue. Inside the cover there is a statement: 'The striking new Titling capitals on our front cover form an advance showing of a new series No.324, called Albertus.' 28.5×22 cm

42

ALBERTVS MAGNVS
Signature, London
No.3, July 1936
The first showing of the complete Albertus Titling alphabet in 72pt appears on the four-page inset between pages 14 and 15. The foreword, A New Titling, states: 'It is obviously a cut, and not a drawn letter, and possesses that squareness which in Roman inscriptions so notably serves legibility; but while true to the orthodox proportions, displays a marked individuality in the treatment of detail. The main strokes so terminate that the alphabet stands midway between the classical inscriptional letter and the modern sanserif.' 25×18.5 cm

43

ALBERTUS BROADSHEET
This titling specimen from 1936 includes a new, wider letter T and the original M, W and ampersand together with new alternative characters. Although it refers to the type as 'cut in seven sizes from 14 to 72 point', only six sizes are in fact displayed. An earlier proof variant in the designer's possession shows two letters in all seven sizes.

At the head of the broadsheet is a roundel with four hounds carrying torches between the arms of a cross, ringed by the word VERITAS. This device was designed by Berthold Wolpe for Stanley Morison. 60×39 cm

44

BROADSHEET
presented to the Albertus Magnus Akademie
in Cologne by the Monotype Corporation
in 1937
The same Latin text about Albert the Great which appeared first in Signature No.3 (but for the ungrammatical 'celebris' which Stanley Morison changed to 'celeber') is set here in 72pt together with the complete alphabet. At the top appears a device of a torch-carrying hound with the word VERITAS, drawn by Wolpe and used again a year later with the first showing of Albertus Text. 63×44 cm

45

ALBERTUS in various sizes
Monotype Recorder, London
Volume 34, No.4, Winter 1936–7
'... Albertus here displays its suitability for posters and headlines of the Coronation Year'
The centre opening displays for the first time four new sizes of Albertus Titling, adding 24, 36,

48 and 60 to the original 72pt size. The type was also used on the cover and on the title page of this issue.   28.5 × 22 cm

46

BROADSHEET

'This is a Printing-Office. Cross-roads of Civilisation. Refuge of all the Arts . . .'
Text by Beatrice Warde

Produced by the Monotype Corporation in 1936, showing Albertus Titling in 18, 24, 36, 48, 60 and 72pt.   59 × 46 cm

47

ALBERTUS TEXT

Signature, London
No.9, July 1938

On page 1 of the preliminaries of this issue, the Monotype Corporation announced: 'A lower case has now been designed and cut as a supplement to the existing titling series 324. The new full fount, "Albertus Text" of which this, the 24 point, is the first specimen, will be known as Series 481.'   25 × 18.5 cm

◆ ALBERTUS CAPITALS ◆

ABCDEFGHIJKLMNOPQ
CUT IN SEVEN SIZES
RSTUVWXYZ!?&MW&
FROM 14 TO 72 POINT
EXCLUSIVELY WITH
MONOTYPE* MACHINES

48

ALBERTUS LIGHT

Charles Baudelaire: Le Soleil
Cambridge, Rampant Lions Press, 1972

Albertus Light, Series 534, was designed by Berthold Wolpe for Monotype in 1939. It was only ever cut in 24pt and is shown here as used by Sebastian Carter at the Rampant Lions Press. 55.5×38 cm

49

ALBERTUS BOLD

Monotype Series 538
Original drawing of the titling in 72pt

The bold version of Albertus was designed by Berthold Wolpe in the spring of 1940. Some sizes were cut by Monotype in the same year.

In September 1940 the 24pt was used on the cover of the Monotype Recorder and three months later a complete alphabet of this size appeared in Signature, No.15, together with Sachsenwald and Pegasus as illustrations to an article by Nicolete Gray on the work of the designer.

Lent by the Monotype Corporation

15.2×20.2 cm

50

OSCAR WILDE

La Ballade de la Geôle de Reading
The Ballad of Reading Gaol
by C.3.3. [Oscar Wilde]
Paris, Raymond Gid, 1980

The main French text is in 24pt Albertus, accompanied by the original English verses in a reduced size (about 9pt) of Albertus Light not found in the Monotype series. The French translation was made, set by hand and decorated with an original lithograph by Raymond Gid. Specimen pages had already been shown accompanying an essay by Gid, 'De Qualité', in Bibliophiles, No.2, 1974.

Limited edition of 200 copies on 'Arches' mould made paper. 24.3×22 cm

51

NEW YEAR BOOKLET

containing a poem by Marguerite de Navarre
Paris, Hachette, 1962

The poem is set in 14pt Albertus. Of special interest is the imprint in a reduced size (approximately 8pt) of Albertus: 'Typographie manuelle d'Union Elysées en charactères Albertus et en Diane'. 20×11 cm

ALBERTUS
ALBERTUS

HYPERION

nach Entwürfen von Berthold Wolpe in 12 Graden gegossen

52

HYPERION
nach Entwürfen von Berthold Wolpe
in 12 Graden gegossen
Frankfurt am Main, Bauersche Giesserei,
c.1950

This type, an italic in its own right without an accompanying roman, was designed by Berthold Wolpe in 1932 and one size (pica) was cut by Paul Koch, son of Rudolf Koch. It was taken into the range of the Bauer Foundry shortly thereafter but not made available for general commercial use until after the Second World War. The matrices are now held by Fundícion Tipografica Neufville, Barcelona, who issue the type under the name Homero.

This four-page type specimen shows the 6, 8, 9, 10, 12, 14, 16, 20, 24, 28, 36 and 48pt sizes. The pocket in the cover contains a further eighteen pieces in different formats which display Hyperion in a variety of applications including a four-page booklet with a text from Paracelsus.

27 × 19.5 cm

53

ARISTOPHANES
Die Vögel des Aristophanes
Frankfurt am Main, Bauersche Giesserei, 1940

A new translation of THE BIRDS, with full-page colour illustrations by Karel Slovinsky. The text is set in 14pt Hyperion in its final form but the stage directions in 10pt show an earlier version of some characters. The typography for this beautiful book was designed by Heinrich Jost. It is significant that the Bauer Type Foundry, in commemorating the fifth centenary of Gutenberg's invention of printing from moveable type, used the illustrations of a Czech artist and the printing types of a designer who had been proscribed by the then rulers of Germany.

The imprint states that Hyperion was used here for the first time. It had, however, already appeared in HANDWERKERZEICHEN, 1936 and SCHMUCKSTÜCKE UND MARKEN, 1938. This copy is No.117 of an edition of 125.

35 × 27 cm

54

AUS DEN GEBETEN ISRAELS
Übersetzung von Dr Max Dienemann
Offenbach am Main, Siegfried Guggenheim, 1948

Set in 14pt Hyperion and printed on Zerkall, Renker und Söhne's Büttenpapier, by the Bauersche Giesserei, Frankfurt am Main.

27 × 19.5 cm

ICH ANGELOBE DICH MIR AUF IMMER, ICH
angelobe Dich mir durch Gerechtigkeit und durch Recht
und durch Liebe und durch Erbarmen. Und ich angelobe
Dich mir durch Treue und Du wirst IHN erkennen.

O HERR DER WELT, DER KÖNIG SCHON WAR,
eh irgend ein Geschöpf erschaffen ward! Als durch seinen
Willen das All entstanden war da wurde König er genannt.
Und wenn in künftiger Zeit das All vergeht, auch dann wird
er noch König sein, er allein als der Erhabene. Er war, er
ist, und er wird sein in Herrlichkeit. Er ist einzig, und kein
Zweiter ist, der ihm zu vergleichen oder ihm zuzugesellen
wäre. Ohne Anfang ist er und ohne Ende, sein ist die Macht
und Herrschaft. Er ist mein Gott und mein lebendiger Erlöser,
mein Hort und mein Teil in der Zeit der Not. Er ist meine
Fahne und meine Zuflucht, mein Kelch, so oft ich zu ihm
rufe. In seine Hand befehle ich meinen Geist, ob ich schlafe
oder wache. Und mit dem Geist auch meinen Leib, ER ist
mit mir, ich fürchte nichts.

MEIN GOTT, DIE SEELE, DIE DU MIR GEGEBEN
hast, ist rein. Du hast sie geschaffen, Du hast sie gebildet,
Du hast sie mir eingehaucht, Du behütest sie in mir, Du
wirst sie einst von mir nehmen und sie mir wieder zurück=

7

TEMPEST TITLING

55

TEMPEST TITLING
designed by Berthold Wolpe at the Fanfare
Press in 1935

A leaf from the Fanfare Press type specimen
book. It shows the 48 and 60pt sizes of this type
which was cut by Monotype in 1936 for the
exclusive use of the Fanfare Press.
Printed in black and red   34×21.5 cm

56

TEMPEST TITLING
Typography. No.2, Spring 1937
Edited by Robert Harling
London, Shenval Press

On pages 33–35 five type faces are shown,
amongst them Tempest. Four sample lines are
accompanied by the following text:
Tempest was cut to the design of Berthold
Wolpe for Ernest Ingham of the Fanfare Press.
In a note from Mr Ingham concerning the type,
he says: 'Tempest originated from lettering
primarily done for a book-jacket which was so
effective that it was decided to experiment

further with the complete alphabet. After many
adjustments of the letters to suit all combinations of words, the alphabet was passed to the
Monotype Corporation for cutting. It was my
desire to have a type for book-jackets and
broadsides which was completely divorced from
the formal but rather static sans italics so much
in vogue. The curves to the horizontals explain
themselves. They add a sense of movement and
a feeling of urgency to the words.'   28×23 cm

57

TEMPEST BROADSHEET
dedicated to the Bauer Type Foundry

'To Georg Hartmann on the occasion of the
centenary of the Bauersche Giesserei, 1837–
1937. Text from Shakespeare's Tempest; set in
Tempest type designed by Berthold Wolpe for
the Fanfare Press. Printed in London under the
direction of Ernest Ingham.'

Heading set in 60pt Tempest followed by
eight lines from the play in 48pt. At the head of
the broadsheet is the Hartmann coat of arms
printed in red and rendered by B.W. for this
occasion.   89.5×58.2 cm

& FANFARE

58

BERTHOLD WOLPE
A Book of Fanfare Ornaments
With an introduction by James Laver
London, Fanfare Press 1939

Ernest Ingham, the founder of the Fanfare Press, persuaded Berthold Wolpe to supplement the conventional fleurons with modern designs. With this commission in mind, Wolpe designed a series of type ornaments from 1935 onwards. A selection of these was cut in 1936 and matrices were struck from which a supply was cast. In this book, Wolpe composed the units into borders, patterns and decorative tail-pieces and made them up into pages. The entire book, with the Tempest type used on the title page, is his own design and it was completed by Christmas 1938, but only a unique copy bears this date.

From James Laver's introduction: 'Yet the little bits of metal which are the notes of the printer's keyboard can be cut to many shapes, and there is no reason why their number should be arbitrarily limited to twenty-six, or to fifty-two, plus comma, colon, and full-stop ... yet there is no reason why he should not sometimes take a holiday and amuse himself with printable projections on metal which are decorative units and nothing else.

'Where shall he find such decorative units? Shall he go back to the printers' ornaments of earlier ages, or shall he employ an artist (one who understands typography and finds a volupté in the very smell of printers' ink) to devise for him new shapes with which to construct new patterns?' 29×22 cm

59

FILM TITLES
Using his Fanfare Ornaments, Berthold Wolpe designed three titles for the film 'Britain Can Make It', a production of the Central Office of Information in 1946. 23×32 cm

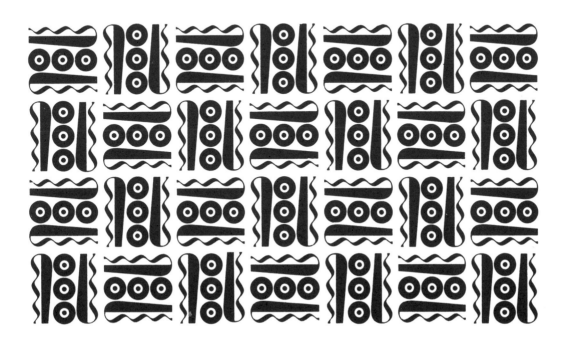

60

THE HOLY BIBLE

Genesis, I, 1 and II, 1–12

Berthold Wolpe's contribution to LIBER LIBRORUM, an international project to celebrate in 1955 the fifth centenary of the Gutenberg 42-line Bible

The imprint states: 'The text type of these pages is Pegasus, cut in 1938 by the Monotype Corporation; cast, set & printed by the Westerham Press. Headings & initials are set in Monotype Albertus and Westerham Press Decorata.'

In 1937 Stanley Morison asked Berthold Wolpe to design a book-face printing type to be produced by the Monotype Corporation. In response to this request Wolpe designed a type, to be called Pegasus, between September and November 1937. Morison approved the design and this roman type, Monotype Series 508, was cut in 16pt in 1938.

The first trial proof of a few characters is dated 30 May 1938. Morison in an accompanying letter asked Wolpe for approval 'to permit our cutting the rest of the fount, so as to complete with the least possible delay'. The fount was completed and proofed by 23 July 1938. The numerals, however, were not cut before July 1939 in spite of the fact that two sets of numerals had been supplied with the original design. In a note dated 3 July 1939 Morison asked Wolpe for his observations on the numerals and the accented sorts. In August 1940 Monotype printed a specimen page of Pegasus for their type specimen book. The 16pt remained the only size available till now.

33 × 22 cm

61

TED HUGHES

Crow: from the Life and Songs of the Crow
With twelve drawings by Leonard Baskin
London, Faber & Faber, 1973

The book was designed by Berthold Wolpe and shows the use of his Pegasus type. It was set by hand and printed on T. H. Saunders mould-made paper at the John Roberts Press under the guidance of Bernard Roberts.

The copy shown is No.'A' of an edition limited to 400 copies signed by the author and illustrator. 33.5 × 24.5 cm

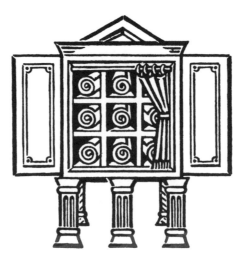

THE FIRST BOOK OF MOSES CALLED

GENESIS

CHAPTER I

IN the beginning God created the heaven and the earth. 2 And the earth was without form, and void; and darkness was upon the face of the deep. And the Spirit of God moved upon the face of the waters. 3 And God said, Let there be light: and there was light. 4 And God saw the light, that it was good: and God divided the light from the darkness. 5 And God called the light Day, and the darkness he called Night. And the evening and the morning were the first day.

¶ 6 And God said, Let there be a firmament in the midst of the waters, and let it divide the waters from the waters. 7 And God made the firmament, and divided the waters which were under the firmament from the waters which were above the firmament: and it was so. 8 And God called the firmament Heaven. And the evening and the morning were the second day.

¶ 9 And God said, Let the waters under the heaven be gathered together unto one place, and let the dry land appear: and it was so. 10 And God called the dry land Earth; and the gathering together of the waters called he Seas: and God saw that it was good. 11 And God said, Let the earth bring forth grass, the herb yielding seed, and the fruit tree yielding fruit after his kind, whose seed is in itself, upon the earth: and it was so. 12 And the earth brought forth grass, and herb yielding seed after his kind, and the tree yielding fruit, whose seed was in itself, after his kind:

Sachsenwald-Gotisch

62

A BLACK-LETTER BROADSIDE

Sachsenwald-Gotisch type specimen from 1937 showing eight sizes from 12 to 72pt

The German text, and the arms of the Bismarck family, specially cut for this issue, are printed in black in a frame made up of type in red. 57×44 cm

63

SACHSENWALD

Monotype Recorder, London
Volume 36, No.1, Spring 1937

The front and back covers of this issue introduce Sachsenwald Gothic, Monotype Series 457. Berthold Wolpe's design had originally been known as Bismarck Schrift. The entire number is devoted to gothic type and Stanley Morison wrote an article for it entitled 'Black letter: its origin & current use', to mark the first showing of Sachsenwald. 28.5×22 cm

64

SACHSENWALD GOTHIC

Signature, London
No.8, March 1938

A small folio specimen sheet of Sachsenwald Gothic type, 14 to 72pt, designed by B.W. for the Monotype Corporation. This sheet was an insert to Signature, which contains the following note on p.53:

'The appearance of the face created unusual interest in this country amongst horizon-scanning advertisers and accordingly certain alternative capitals were cut to carry out still further the romanization of the letter in the interest of Anglo-Saxon eyes. There is a possibility that, succeeding the exhaustion of the novelty-value of one after another of the nineteenth-century jobbing categories such as sans, egyptian, etc., there may follow a passing vogue in advertising display for the only remaining unexplored group: black letter. If so, it will certainly not be the English black-letter associated with religious announcements, but a simple and compact and new black-letter such as this.

'There are few typographers who would not be tempted by the opportunity this face offers of massing bold letters, which are nevertheless free of the bloated effect of any roman expanded into an extra bold weight.' 35×22 cm

65

RUBAIYAT OF OMAR KHAYYAM

rendered in English Verse
by Edward Fitzgerald
The text of the first edition
illustrated by Arthur Szyk
New York, The Heritage Club, 1940

Page proofs. The colophon of the book states: 'The text was set, and the pages made-up in English Monotype Sachsenwald with Albertus Capitals ... under the Direction of Ernest Ingham at the Fanfare Press, in London.'

29×21 cm

In principio erat verbum

O thou beneficent ART & MYSTERY whose mission it is to carry Enlightenment to all people from age to age: Make us, thy craftsmen, worthy of thee and of all the craftsmen who in times past have glorified thee. Let thy light shine upon our lives and upon our vocations. May no word of ours, or any of our handiwork, bring dishonour upon thee; but rather may we uphold thy dignity at all times and in all places, and in brotherly love and helpfulness advance thy fame, to the end that all men may be persuaded to acknowledge thee as Mightiest among the Arts and Crafts So let it be!

XLVIII

While the Rose blows along the River Brink,
With old Khayyám the Ruby Vintage drink:
   And when the Angel with his darker Draught
Draws up to Thee — take that, and do not shrink.

XLIX

'Tis all a Chequer-board of Nights and Days
Where Destiny with Men for Pieces plays:
   Hither and thither moves, and mates, and slays,
And one by one back in the Closet lays.

L

The Ball no Question makes of Ayes and Noes,
But Right or Left as strikes the Player goes;
   And He that toss'd Thee down into the Field,
He knows about it all — HE knows — HE knows!

LI

The Moving Finger writes; and, having writ,
Moves on: nor all thy Piety nor Wit
   Shall lure it back to cancel half a Line,
Nor all thy Tears wash out a Word of it.

66

DECORATA

Sacheverell Sitwell and Wilfred Blunt:
Great Flower Books, 1700–1900
London, Collins, 1956

The jacket and title page of this book, which was designed by Ruari McLean, show the first use of Berthold Wolpe's Decorata.

An alphabet of these foliated letters was subsequently completed for use at Rowley Atterbury's Westerham Press.

49.5×35 cm

67

LTB ITALIC

An italic sanserif type to go with Edward Johnston's London Transport type

The original drawing of capital and lower case alphabets designed by Berthold Wolpe in 1973. He was commissioned to design this italic and was asked to match the existing Johnston sanserif roman. The resulting alphabets were carefully designed to do this but also to be economical and space-saving.

20×51 cm

ABCDEFG
abcdefghik

LTB ITALIC

PRINTING PRESSES

HISTORY AND DEVELOPMENT
FROM THE FIFTEENTH
CENTURY TO MODERN TIMES

JAMES MORAN

FABER AND FABER LIMITED
3 QUEEN SQUARE LONDON

Book-design and Typography

The titles in this section are of Faber books which have been seen through the press by Berthold Wolpe. He was responsible for their typography, binding and jackets.

68
PAUL KLEE
On Modern Art
London, Faber & Faber, 1948
Set in Walbaum and printed at the Curwen Press, Plaistow.   21 × 22.5 cm

69
GEOFFREY KEYNES
William Blake's Engravings
London, Faber & Faber, 1950
Set in Walbaum and printed at the Shenval Press, Hertford.
Shown at National Book League Design Exhibition.   25.5 × 19.5 cm

70
TALBOT BAINES REED
A History of the Old English Letter Foundries
With notes historical and bibliographical on the rise and progress of English typography
A new edition revised and enlarged
by A. F. Johnson
London, Faber & Faber, 1952
Set in Bell with initials in Caslon and printed at the University Press, Oxford.   28 × 19 cm

71
MARCEL ROUFF
The Passionate Epicure
London, Faber & Faber, 1961
With illustrations by Charles Mozley
Set in Bell, Gresham and Marina Script and printed by W. & J. Mackay, Chatham.
22 × 16 cm

72
ALEC DAVIS
Package and Print
The Development of Container and Label Design
London, Faber & Faber, 1967
Set in Bulmer and Gresham and printed by W. & J. Mackay, Chatham.   28.5 × 22.2 cm

73
A. S. OSLEY
Mercator: A monograph on the lettering of maps, etc., in the 16th century Netherlands with a facsimile and translation of his treatise on the italic hand and a translation of Ghim's
VITA MERCATORIS
London, Faber & Faber, 1969
Set in Ehrhardt and Caslon and printed at the University Press, Oxford.   29 × 22 cm

BERTHOLDO WOLPE

TYPOGRAPHO VALDE DOCTO

NOVORVM ALBERTI CHARACTERVM

INVENTORI

AMICO FIDELISSIMO

HVNC DEDICAT AVCTOR LIBRVM

Dedication by the author of MERCATOR

74

JAMES MORAN
Printing Presses
History and Development from the Fifteenth
Century to Modern Times
London, Faber & Faber, 1973
Set in Modern No.7 and Victoria Titling and
printed at the University Press, Oxford.
27 × 18.5 cm

75

NICOLETE GRAY
Nineteenth Century Ornamented Typefaces
With a chapter on Ornamented Types in
America by Ray Nash
London, Faber & Faber, 1976

The chart of ornamented types was prepared
by Nicholas Biddulph.
Set in Times Roman, Victoria and Thorne
Shaded and printed at the University Press,
Oxford.   28.5 × 22 cm

76

TED HUGHES
Cave Birds: an Alchemical Cave Drama
Poems by Ted Hughes and
drawings by Leonard Baskin
London, Faber & Faber, 1978
Set in Times Roman and Albertus and printed
at the Scolar Press, Ilkley.   23 × 28.5 cm

MERCATOR

A monograph on the lettering of maps, etc.
in the 16th century Netherlands
with a facsimile and translation of
his treatise on the italic hand
and a translation of Ghim's
VITA MERCATORIS

A. S. OSLEY

With a Foreword by R. A. Skelton

FABER AND FABER
LONDON

Illustrations and Devices

77

NONESUCH PRESS
Selected Poems of Coleridge
London, The Nonesuch Press, 1935
This book was edited by Stephen Potter and designed by Francis Meynell. 500 copies were printed at the Fanfare Press on Auvergne hand-made paper.
Three illustrations by Stefan Mrozewski.
Title-page design by Berthold Wolpe.

29 × 18 cm

Limited edition of 200 copies printed under the direction of James Wardrop. Several artists worked on the embellishment of this book: Alfred Fairbank designed the lettering and initials, Reynolds Stone the coats of arms and Wolpe the two maps.

The book was selected to be among the Fifty Books exhibited by the First Edition Club in 1937. This was the predecessor of the National Book League Book Design Exhibition.

35 × 24 cm

79

STEFAN ZWEIG
Der Begrabene Leuchter
Mit Zeichnungen von Berthold Wolpe
Vienna, Herbert Reichner, 1937
Stefan Zweig had come to live in London and asked Wolpe to illustrate his text. The fourteen designs are printed in brownish red ink. The tail-piece, which shows a dove with an olive branch perched on a spade against the setting sun, is signed and dated: 'BLW del 1937'.

22 × 14.5 cm

78

GREGYNOG PRESS
John, Lord of Joinville, Seneschal
of Champagne
The History of Saint Louis
Translated by Joan Evans
Newtown, The Gregynog Press, 1937

80

STEFAN ZWEIG
The Buried Candelabrum
Translated by Eden and Cedar Paul
New York, The Viking Press, 1937
This American edition has the same illustrations as the item above. 23 × 14.5 cm

81

STEFAN ZWEIG
Legende
La leggende della terza colomba, Il candelabro sepolto, Gli occhi dell'eterno fratello, Rachele contende con Dio
Milan, Sperling & Kupfer, 1937
This book contains five new illustrations as well as the designs shown in the Reichner and Viking editions of THE BURIED CANDELABRUM.

In addition to the ordinary edition in paper covers, a hundred copies were printed on special paper with prints of the illustrations mounted on blank leaves. This copy, No. 19, is signed by author and artist.   24×15 cm

82

STEFAN ZWEIG

George Frederick Handel's Resurrection /
Auferstehung Georg Friedrich Händels
[London] Corvinus Press, 1938

The Corvinus Press was established by Viscount Carlow in the mid-thirties and its last publication appeared in 1945. Viscount Carlow himself was killed while serving with the RAF during the Second World War. The book was hand-set in Rudolf Koch's Marathon type and printed on Zanders hand-made paper, in an edition of thirty copies. The copy shown is No. 24. Wolpe designed the title-page, two decorated initials, two tail-pieces, the phoenix device on the title-page also blocked in gold on the front board and the Corvinus Press emblem blocked on the back board. 28 × 20 cm

83

MAGNA CARTA
and other Charters of English Liberties
With head and tail pieces by Berthold Wolpe
London, Guyon House Press, 1938

Vivian Ridler printed these texts with translations by Noël Denholm-Young. F. J. Coton was the binder and Theodore Besterman the publisher after whose house the press was named. The edition comprised 250 copies but over half of them were destroyed, together with the press at Bunhill Row in the City of London, during the war.

Copies A-F were printed on vellum and one of these was shown in the Library of Congress together with an original charter when the latter was sent to the United States for safe keeping during the war. The remaining copies were printed on Batchelor hand-made paper. Albertus was used on the title page and for charter titles. It was the first use of this type in a printed book.

a. Copy No.126 on paper   30 × 22 cm
    Lent by the executors of the late
    Theodore Besterman:

b. Copy No.A on vellum

c. Bound volume containing original drawings

HENRICVS

KINGJOHN

KENNETH MACRAE MOIR
*Some Adventures of a Cornet of Horse
in the Crimean War.*
A paper read before the Sette of Odd
Volumes at its 526th meeting on
22 November 1938
London, The Sette of Odd Volumes, 1938

Printed in 177 copies at the Fanfare Press. The
hand-coloured decorations by Berthold Wolpe
include the cover design, title-page border and
three vignettes.
Typography by Arnold Jones.

15 × 11.5 cm

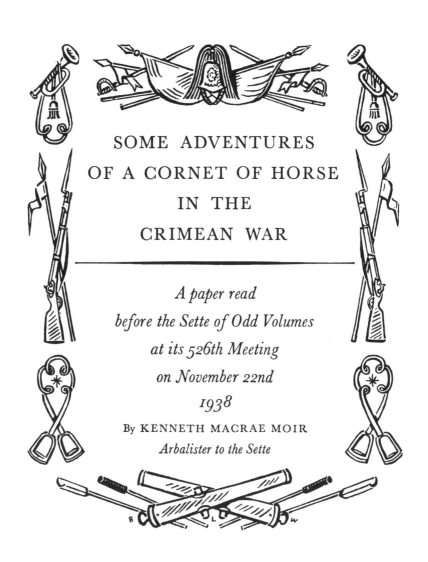

85

CHODERLOS DE LACLOS

Dangerous Acquaintances
Les Liaisons Dangereuses
Englished by Ernest Dowson, the preface by
André Gide, the illustrations by Chas Laborde
London, Nonesuch Press, 1940
Francis Meynell asked Berthold Wolpe to draw
character figurines to be printed as letter-heads
which would help the reader to identify the
writers and recipients of the letters which make
up this book. The binding cloth is also Wolpe's
design.

a. Wolpe's own copy is inscribed 'with
gratitude and admiration' by Francis Meynell.

b. 'The characters in epistolary order': proof on
india paper of the figurines.   23.5 × 17.5 cm

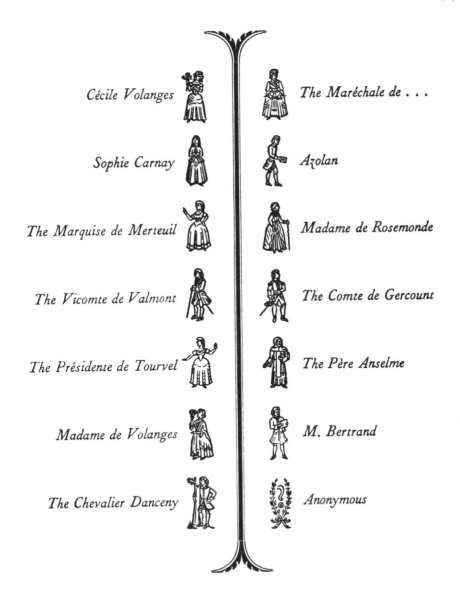

Cécile Volanges

Sophie Carnay

The Marquise de Merteuil

The Vicomte de Valmont

The Présidente de Tourvel

Madame de Volanges

The Chevalier Danceny

The Maréchale de . . .

Azolan

Madame de Rosemonde

The Comte de Gercount

The Père Anselme

M. Bertrand

Anonymous

86

WALTER DE LA MARE
Collected Poems
With decorations by Berthold Wolpe
London, Faber & Faber, 1942

Berthold Wolpe made twelve drawings for this
volume in 1941. Not all the designs refer to
particular poems but they are generally
intended to indicate the mood of the sections
into which the book is divided. The jacket and
the binding are also Wolpe's work.

20.5 × 14.5 cm

87

WALTER DE LA MARE

A typed note referring to Wolpe's illustrations
for Collected Poems, with holograph postscript:
'I am looking forward so much to seeing his
designs'.
Signed: W J d l m and dated: 15 XII 41.

25.5 × 19 cm

88

WALTER DE LA MARE
Collected Rhymes & Verses
With decorations by Berthold Wolpe
London, Faber & Faber, 1944
As a result of the war-time economy drive to save paper, the decorations were conceived as border-pieces for the section titles. The jacket and the hard-cover binding were also Wolpe's design.

20.5 × 14.5 cm

89

F. LE MESURIER
Sauces French and English
With drawings by Berthold Wolpe
London, Faber & Faber, 1947

An enlarged version of the illustration from page 11 is repeated on the bookjacket.

19 × 13 cm

Sauce for the goose

is Sauce for the Gander

90

NELL HEATON
Traditional Recipes of the British Isles.
With drawings by Berthold and
Margaret Wolpe
London, Faber & Faber, 1951

The hard-cover binding and the jacket are by Wolpe.

22 × 16 cm

91

COMMEMORATIVE DEVICE
for Karl Klingspor

In 1938 Stanley Morison commissioned Wolpe to produce a design to commemorate the seventieth birthday of Dr Karl Klingspor, the distinguished German type-founder. The device shows a gothic letter 'k', reversed, in white, as on a printing type and then in black on white, as though printed from the former. The acorns and oak leaves relate to the town of Offenbach, the coat of arms of which has an oak tree as its main feature. The spurs are an allusion to the honorant's family name.

92

PELICAN HISTORY OF ART
Device of the 'Pelican in her Piety'

Designed by Berthold Wolpe in 1953 for the Pelican History of Art, edited by Nikolaus Pevsner and published by Penguin Books Ltd, Harmondsworth. This device, in a smaller size is blocked in gold on the front boards of the books in the series. It also appears on their title-pages and jackets. 7.5×6 cm

a. The block proof reflects the original intention of the designer.
b. The title-page of 'Ein neuentdeckter Modus Scribendi ...' shows the device in its final use, printed in red and black. The first printed edition of this original ms. was issued by Morison and dedicated to Karl Klingspor. 6×3.4 cm

93

EURIPIDES
The Bacchae and other plays
Translated by Philip Vellacott
Harmondsworth, Penguin Books, 1954
Original drawing by Berthold Wolpe for decoration on the front cover. 9.5×6.5 cm

94

NIKOLAUS PEVSNER
The Buildings of England
Original drawings by Berthold Wolpe of
roundels for front-cover decorations of
two books in this Penguin series

a. London I: The Cities of London
   and Westminster. 1957   diameter 8 cm
b. South and West Somerset. 1958
                              diameter 9 cm

95

SUETONIUS
The Twelve Caesars
translated by Robert Graves
Harmondsworth, Penguin Books, 1957
The roundel which appears on the front cover
as well as the coin portraits which appear at the
head of each chapter were drawn by Berthold
Wolpe. A copy of this book was included in the
British Book Design Exhibition 1959.
                              18 × 11 cm

96

COATS OF ARMS

a. Coat of arms of the family of
Johannes Gutenberg
This version was first used in Signature, No.14,
May 1940 and appeared on the cover of the
Monotype Recorder, Special Number, Sept.
1940   13.5 × 12 cm

b. Coat of arms of the Theatre Royal, Bristol
A rendering of the arms of George III, in whose
reign the theatre was built. In the war years the
theatre was managed by CEMA, the forerunner
of the present Arts Council. The design was
used on posters and play-bills printed at the
Curwen Press. 1942   25 × 20 cm

c. Coat of arms of John Henry Cardinal
Newman (1801–1890)
for 'Homage to Newman:
1845–1945',
London, 1945   23 × 25 cm

IN MEMORIAM
IOHANNIS
GUTENBERG

97

THE HOLSTEIN PAPERS
Edited by Norman Rich and H. M. Fisher
Vol. 1. Memoirs
Cambridge University Press, 1955
The title page bears the von Holstein arms designed by Berthold Wolpe for the series.

25 × 16 cm

98

OLIVER SIMON
Printer and Playground
An autobiography
London, Faber & Faber, 1956
Oliver Simon dedicated this book to his two children. Berthold Wolpe designed the dedicatory panel: MCM To Jill and Timothy LVI.

8.5 × 6.2 cm

99

FILM TRADE-MARK
Design for
Metro-Goldwyn-Mayer / London Films Ltd
In 1943 Wolpe was commissioned by Vincent Korda to design a title piece for use on the screen and as a trade-mark for the intended union of London Films, Sir Alexander Korda's company, with Metro-Goldwyn-Mayer. The designer remembers a meeting with Korda and with representatives of both companies, during which the device was discussed. As it happened, the union did not last and the device was never used.

33 × 38 cm

100

POETRY LONDON
Colophon designed by Berthold Wolpe
in 1943 for Tambimutu's Poetry London
a. Larger version used on a catalogue cover.

8.5 × 9 cm

b. Original drawing of small version used on title-pages.

1.6 × 1.8 cm

101

COLOPHON
for Faber & Faber
Block proof of a colophon designed for the firm's medical and nursing books. Used on catalogue covers and in advertising display c.1950.

25 × 20 cm

102

LINCOLN CATHEDRAL DEVICE
Reproduction of a drawing of Lincoln Cathedral for the cover of a guide-book designed by Ruari McLean. Also used, in a smaller size, as a colophon for the Lincoln Minster Pamphlets.

7.5 × 6 cm

105

UNIVERSITY OF ESSEX

Official seal and stamp
designed by Berthold Wolpe in 1965

a. and b. Original drawings for seal and stamp in
pen, brush and ink.

diameters 12.5 and 12.3 cm

c. Finished stamp. diameter 3.2 cm

d. A relief impression on paper of the official
seal. The die was engraved by Mr Cavanagh of
Messrs G. T. Friend. diameter 6 cm

103

DEVICE

for the Merrion Press

a. Original drawing of a colophon designed
for Susan (née Mahon) Shaw's Merrion Press,
1959. 3.5×3 cm

b. A gilt metal plaque based on the drawing.
Used on the press's van. 17.5×15 cm

106

WINE AND FOOD SOCIETY

Device designed in 1937 for André Simon

Proofs in red on Japanese paper with two
versions of the design. 25.5×20 cm

104

WILLIAM FAULKNER

Requiem for a Nun
Harmondsworth, Penguin Books in
association with Chatto and Windus, 1960

a. Berthold Wolpe designed a monogram
device with the author's initials, which was used
on the covers of all Faulkner's books in this
series. 18×11 cm

b. A booklet containing thirteen ideas for the
device as submitted to the publisher.

107

DEVICE
for Double Crown Club
A crown of open books: original drawing
Designed for a dinner menu, set in Pegasus type
and printed by Foister and Jagg of Cambridge.
It was again used on a menu in 1975 and
appears, in reduced size, on the note-paper of
the club's present secretary. 1947   25.5 × 20 cm

108

CITY MUSIC SOCIETY
Original drawing of a device for this society in
the City of London.   9 × 7 cm

109

DRAMATIC DEVICE
Design for the Westerham Amateur Dramatic
Society, for use on posters and programmes
c.1950.   10 × 9 cm

110

BOOK PLATE
Original drawing by Berthold Wolpe for
Dr Paul Lazarus. 1934   7.3 × 6.7 cm

111

BOOK PLATE
Heraldic ex libris drawn for the Sykes family
by Berthold Wolpe in 1937.   9 × 5.5 cm

112

BOOK STAMP
Original drawing of a supra ex libris for the
Hirsch Music Library
The drawing was commissioned in 1948, when
the Hirsch Library was transferred to the British
Museum. The design was cut on brass in three
sizes: the largest to be blocked on folios, a
medium size on quartos, and the smallest on
octavo size books.   8 × 7 cm

113

EX LIBRIS
for Montague Shaw
The border has at its base an open book with
blank pages for writing in dates, etc. Designed
by Berthold Wolpe c.1960.   8 × 7 cm

Benjamin Britten

Noye's Fludde

B·L·WOLPE

Book-Jackets, Covers and Bindings

114

J. S. BACH
Seb. Bachs Gesänge
zu G. Chr. Schemellis 'Musicalischem
Gesangbuch' Leipzig 1736.
Mit ausgebreitetem Generalbass
Herausgegeben von Max Seiffert
Kassel, Bärenreiter-Verlag [1935]
Label design by Berthold Wolpe, on coloured
pattern paper.   27 × 19 cm

115

G. PH. TELEMANN
Singe-, Spiel- und Generalbass-Übungen,
Hamburg 1733/34
Herausgegeben von Max Seiffert
Kassel, Bärenreiter-Verlag, 1935
Label design by Wolpe, on coloured pattern
paper.   27 × 19 cm

116

BÉLA BARTÓK
Violin concerto No.1 (op. posth.)
Violin and piano [version]: (Hans-Heinz
Schneeberger)
London, Hawkes & Son [1958]
Cover design by Wolpe: reversed pen lettering
on deep blue ground; the composer's name in
roman, the rest in italic.   31 × 23.5 cm

117

BENJAMIN BRITTEN
Noye's Fludde:
The Chester Miracle Play
London, Hawkes & Son [1958]
Berthold Wolpe designed the cover which in-
cludes a photograph by Kurt Hutton.
                                  31 × 24 cm

118

BENJAMIN BRITTEN
Songs from the Chinese Op.58
For high voice and guitar
The words translated by Arthur Waley
The guitar part edited by Julian Bream
London, Boosey & Co, 1959
Cover design by Wolpe which incorporates a
photographic reproduction of an 11th-century
Chinese painting.   31 × 24 cm

119

ARNOLD SCHOENBERG
String Quartet in D major 1897
edition prepared by O. W. Neighbour
London, Faber Music Ltd, 1966
Cover design by Wolpe, using Albertus type –
reversed to appear white on a blue background.   26.5 × 18.5 cm

120

BENJAMIN BRITTEN
The Poet's Echo / Des Dichters Echo
Six Poems of Pushkin / Sechs Gedichte von Puschkin
for high voice and piano / für hohe Stimme und Klavier. Op.76.
English translation by Peter Pears / deutsche Übersetzung von Hans Keller
London, Faber Music Ltd, 1967
Cover design by Wolpe using Albertus capitals in English and in Russian. Printed in green with lettering reversed in white, including a sepia-tinted photograph of the countryside near Pushkin's birthplace by B. Skobelvuvin.

31 × 23 cm

121

BENJAMIN BRITTEN
Cantata Misericordium
Composed for and first performed at the solemn ceremony on the commemoration day of the centenary of the Red Cross, Geneva September 1st, 1963
London, Boosey & Hawkes [1973]
Wolpe designed two covers for this work:
a. The first one reproduces a rubbing in pastels from the cut lettering.
b. The final version is printed solid in dark green and red.

26.5 × 18.5 cm

122

PETER MAXWELL DAVIES
Vesalii Icones
For dancer, solo cello and instrumental ensemble. Full score
London, Boosey & Hawkes [1978]
Cover designed by Wolpe incorporating a woodcut from Andreas Vesalius DE HUMANIS CORPORIS FABRICA 1543.
Printed in black and red on toned paper.

31 × 23.5 cm

123

OSKAR SCHÜRER
Augsburg
(Deutsche Bauten, 22ster Band)
Burg bei Magdeburg, August Hopfer, 1934

Front cover by Berthold Wolpe. Previous covers in the series 'Deutsche Bauten' were designed by Rudolf Koch.

17 × 12 cm

124

RUDOLF KOCH
Häusliches Leben: Schattenbilder
Leipzig, Insel-Verlag [1934]
Berthold Wolpe's design for the cover consists of a written label on a pattern background.

18.5 × 12 cm

I25

M. D. ANDERSON

Misericords:
Medieval life in English woodcarving
Harmondsworth, Penguin Books, 1954

a. Design, on front and on back cover, by Berthold Wolpe; the small type on the front cover is his Pegasus. Elements of the cover design are repeated on the title-page.

18 × 12.5 cm

b. Original drawing for front board and spine, with a specially drawn King Penguin device on the back board.   18.5 × 25 cm

GOLLANCZ JACKETS

'In the latter part of the thirties Dr Wolpe was with the Fanfare Press, and between 1935 and 1939 he did the lay-out for many of the Gollancz jackets. Victor would send the copy over with some such indication as "Title important – author unimportant – reviewer important", leaving the colour to Fanfare to choose. What is so astonishing about this collaboration is that, though the Gollancz and Fanfare offices were about five minutes' walk apart, the two men never met – and yet Dr Wolpe translated the spirit of Victor's intentions with a staggering degree of skill and understanding. Sometimes, instead of using a standard type, he would devise one of his own, as he did in the case of a novel by Louis Golding called THE PURSUER, in which he wanted to create a type that would give the feeling of flight and pursuit. This type was afterwards cut by Fanfare and dubbed Tempest.'

From GOLLANCZ, THE STORY OF A PUBLISHING HOUSE, 1928–1978 by Sheila Hodges

The following selection of jackets is illustrated:
Louis Golding: The Pursuer, 1935
Phyllis Bentley: Freedom Farewell, 1935
Newton Gayle: Murder at 28:10, 1935
Phoebe Atwood Taylor: Sandbar Sinister, 1935
Milward Kennedy: Sic Transit Gloria, 1936
F. Yeats-Brown: Lancer at Large, 1936
A. J. Cronin: The Citadel, 1937
George Orwell: The Road to Wigan Pier, 1937
H. C. Bayley: This is Mr Fortune, 1938
Henry Allen: Action at Avila, 1938

A NEW ASEY MAYO
DETECTIVE STORY
SANDBAR SINISTER

SANDBAR SINISTER by PHOEBE ATWOOD TAYLOR

7/6

● ● ●

by PHOEBE ATWOOD TAYLOR

"A NEW ASEY MAYO TALE is an event"—Torquemada (Observer). "The best writer of her class in America"—Edward Shanks (John O'London). "Readers pick up a new Asey Mayo book in the certainty that it contains a well-hidden mystery, enlightened by humour and worked out with plenty of action"—Times Literary Supplement.

GOLLANCZ

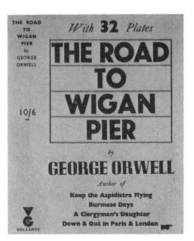

THE ROAD TO WIGAN PIER by GEORGE ORWELL

With 32 Plates
THE ROAD TO WIGAN PIER

10/6

by
GEORGE ORWELL
Author of
Keep the Aspidistra Flying
Burmese Days
A Clergyman's Daughter
Down & Out in Paris & London

GOLLANCZ

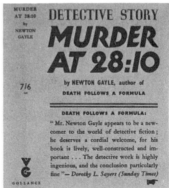

MURDER AT 28:10 by NEWTON GAYLE

DETECTIVE STORY
MURDER AT 28:10

by NEWTON GAYLE, author of
DEATH FOLLOWS A FORMULA

7/6

DEATH FOLLOWS A FORMULA:
"Mr. Newton Gayle appears to be a newcomer to the world of detective fiction; he deserves a cordial welcome, for his book is lively, well-constructed and important . . . The detective work is highly ingenious, and the conclusion particularly fine"—Dorothy L. Sayers (Sunday Times)

GOLLANCZ

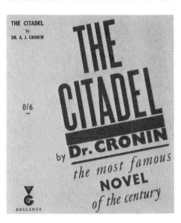

THE CITADEL by DR. A. J. CRONIN

THE CITADEL
by **Dr. CRONIN**

8/6

the most famous
NOVEL
of the century

GOLLANCZ

FREEDOM, FAREWELL! by PHYLLIS BENTLEY

FREEDOM, FAREWELL!

8/6

the new NOVEL by
PHYLLIS BENTLEY
author of
INHERITANCE
A MODERN TRAGEDY
ETC

GOLLANCZ

THIS IS MR. FORTUNE by H. C. BAILEY

THIS IS MR. FORTUNE

7/6

new detective Stories by
H. C. BAILEY

GOLLANCZ

ACTION AT AQUILA by HERVEY ALLEN

ACTION AT AQUILA
BY
HERVEY ALLEN
AUTHOR OF
ANTHONY ADVERSE

8/6

OVER ONE MILLION SOLD
THROUGHOUT THE WORLD

GOLLANCZ

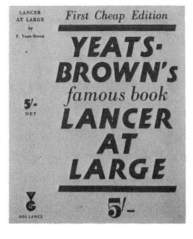

LANCER AT LARGE by F. Yeats-Brown

First Cheap Edition
YEATS-BROWN'S
famous book
LANCER AT LARGE

5/-
NET

5/-

GOLLANCZ

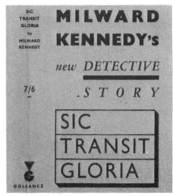

SIC TRANSIT GLORIA by MILWARD KENNEDY

MILWARD KENNEDY's
new DETECTIVE
. S T O R Y

7/6

SIC TRANSIT GLORIA

GOLLANCZ

127

DRAWINGS

in indian ink by Berthold Wolpe for some Faber book jackets

a. D. M. Crook: Spitfire Pilot. 1942

b. Ambrose Heath: Good Food Again. 1950

The jacket design is blocked on the binding.

21 × 13.5 cm

c. Wilson Harris: Palace of the Peacock. 1960

20.5 × 16.5 cm

d. Sylvia Plath: Crossing the Water. 1971

28 × 22 cm

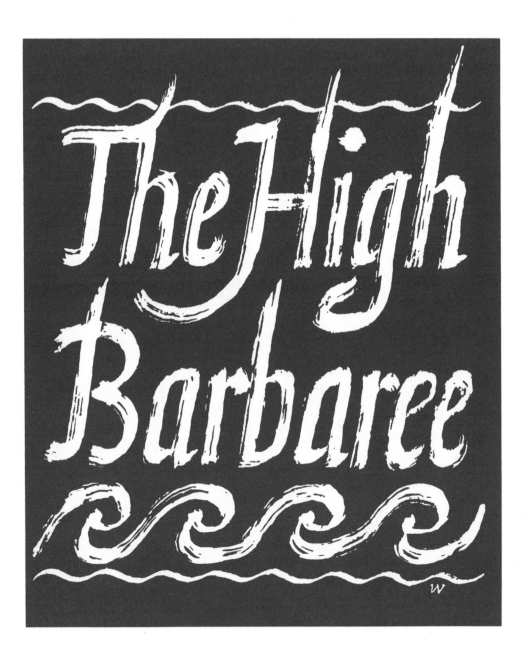

128

BLOCK PROOFS

of title pieces for Faber jackets

a. Nordhoff & Hall: The High Barbaree. 1946

25 × 19 cm

b. Best Ghost Stories. c.1960   11.5 × 10.5 cm

129

FABER JACKETS AND COVERS

There is room to show a mere handful of the more than 1500 jackets and covers Berthold Wolpe designed during his years at Faber and Faber. Those chosen, more or less at random, to be illustrated on plates G & H are:

Michael Graham: The Fish Gate, 1943
Adrian Stokes: Smooth and Rough, 1951
Maurice Collis: Into Hidden Burma, 1953
George N. Patterson: Tibetan Journey, 1954
Amos Tutuola: Simbi & the Satyr of the Dark Jungle, 1955
Jacques Lanzman: The American Rat, 1959
Harold E. Johnson: Sibelius, 1960
Lawrence Durrell: The Dark Labyrinth, 1961
T. S. Eliot: Collected Plays, 1962
Robert Lowell: Imitations, 1962
T. S. Eliot: Collected Poems 1909–1962, 1963
T. S. Eliot: To Criticise the Critic, 1965
William Golding: The Spire, 1965
Alfred Duggan: The Little Emperors, 1968
Richard Murphy: The Battle of Aughrim, 1968
Vernon Watkins: Fidelities, 1968
Seamus Heaney: Door into the Dark, 1969
Thom Gunn: Jack Straw's Castle, 1976

130

FABER BINDINGS

When Berthold Wolpe joined Faber in 1941 the firm's books were conspicuous for the quality and style of their bindings which were largely the work of Richard de la Mare. As well as designing jackets, Wolpe made his own contribution to the bindings hidden behind them. Those illustrated on plate F are:

Sacheverell Sitwell:
    Primitive Scenes and Festivals, 1942
Anthony Rhodes: Sword of Bone, 1942
David Scott: Corporal Jack, 1943
Oriel Malet: Marjory Fleming, 1946
Maurice Collis: Lord of the Three Worlds, 1947
Forrest Reid: Apostate, 1947
Tribute to Walter de la Mare, 1948
Otto Pächt:
    The Master of Mary of Burgundy, 1948
Nell Heaton & André Simon:
    A Calendar of Food and Wine, 1949
Paul Nash: Outline, An Autobiography, 1949
James Fergusson: Lowland Lairds, 1949
Maurice Collis: The Grand Peregrination, 1949
Sir James Fergusson:
    Argyll in the Forty-Five, 1951
W. J. Lawrence:
    No.5 Bomber Group RAF, 1951
T. B. Reed edited by A. F. Johnson: A History of the Old English Letter Foundries, 1952
David A. Embury:
    The Fine Art of Mixing Drinks, 1953
Le Corbusier: The Modulor, 1954
George N. Patterson: Tibetan Journey, 1954
A. J. B. Hutchings: The Baroque Concerto, 1956
R. A. Weigert: French Tapestry, 1956
Lawrence Durrell: Justine, 1957
Ed. by John Betjeman and Geoffrey Taylor:
    English Love Poems, 1957
Richard Southern:
    The Medieval Theatre in the Round, 1957
Amos Tutuola:
    The Brave African Huntress, 1958
Le Corbusier: Modular 2, 1958
Lawrence Durrell: Mountolive, 1958
Lawrence Durrell: Balthazar, 1958

131

CATALOGUE COVER

Faber & Faber, Spring 1942

This was the first catalogue cover designed by
Berthold Wolpe for the firm.   18 × 12 cm

132

COVER DRAWING

Faber Books, Autumn 1948

Original drawing in indian ink for catalogue
cover.   30 × 19.5 cm

133

CATALOGUE COVERS

for Faber & Faber

Eight covers printed from designs and drawings
by Berthold Wolpe
Spring 1948
Spring & Summer 1950
Spring & Summer 1951
Spring & Summer 1952
Books for the Young [n.d.]
Spring & Summer 1953
Autumn & Winter 1955
Spring & Summer [n.d.]   21.5 × 14.5 cm

E

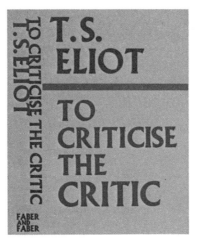

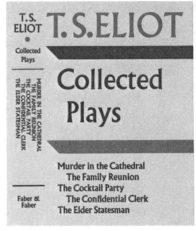

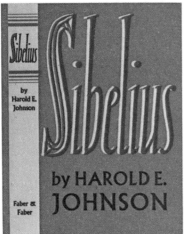

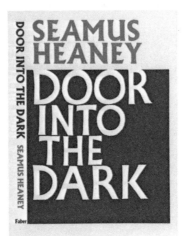

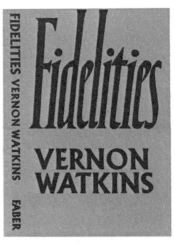

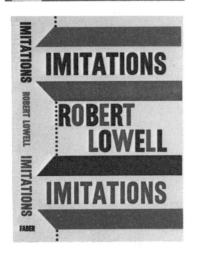

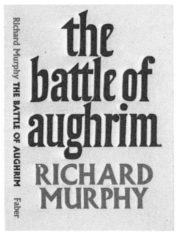

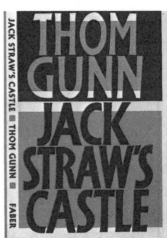

F

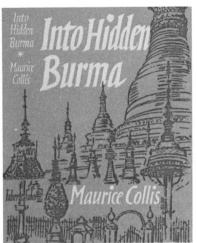

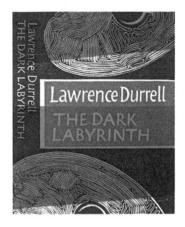

G

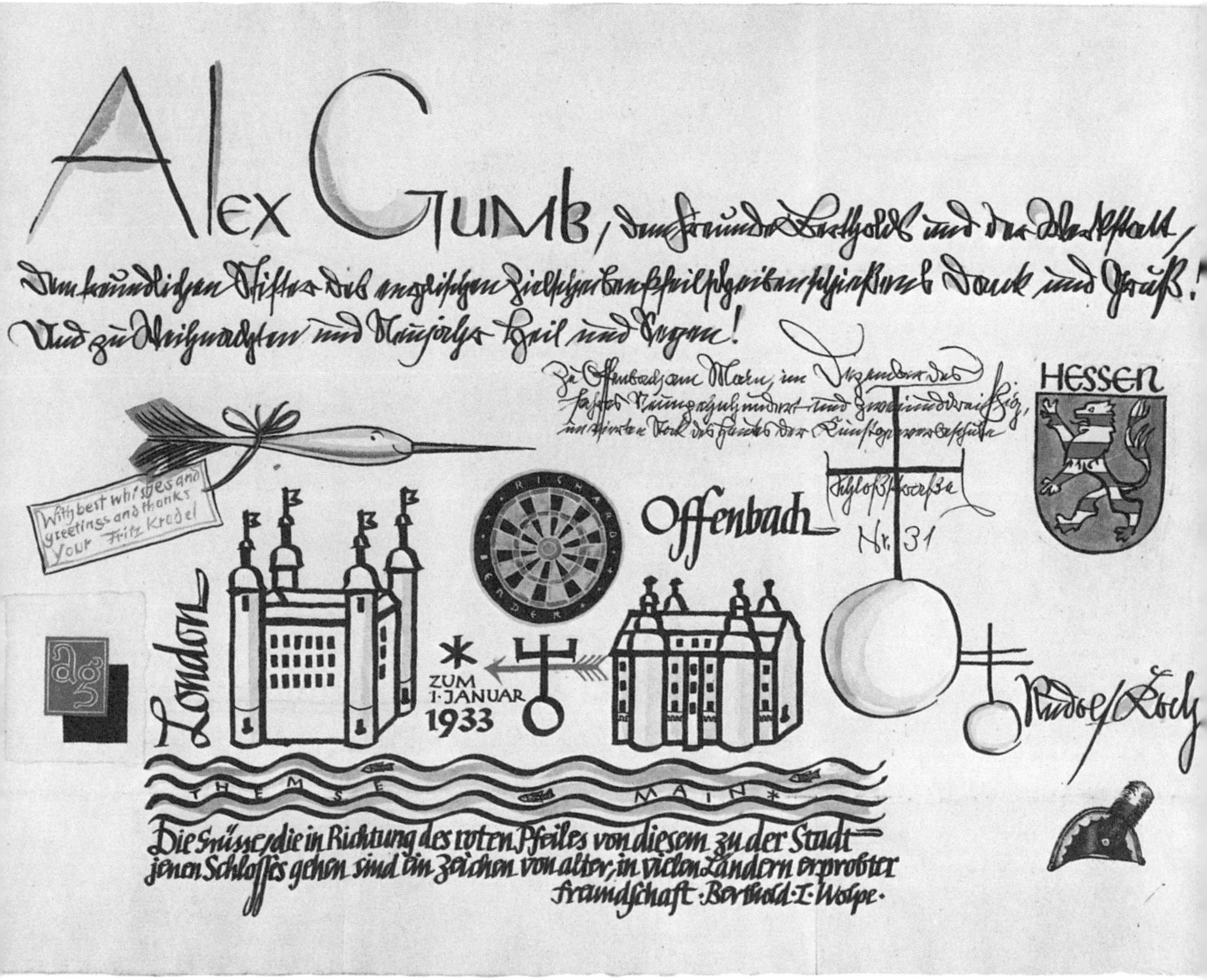

Alex Gumb,

HESSEN

Offenbach

Hr. 31

London

ZUM
1·JANUAR
1933

THEMSE   MAIN

Die Nüsse, die in Richtung des roten Pfeiles von diesem zu der Stadt
jenen Schlosses gehen sind ein Zeichen von alter, in vielen Ländern erprobter
Freundschaft · Berthold L. Wolpe.

H

Die Neue Sammlung
Prinzregentenstraße 3

DIE OFFENBACHER
WERKSTATT

Rudolf koch
fritz kredel · karl Vollmer
Berthold Wolpe u · a ·

---

13 · April – 4 · Mai
Sonntags: 9 – 13 Uhr
Dienstag – Samstag
9 – 16<u>30</u> Eintritt 50 ₰

A Show of Hands

AN EXHIBITION
by the Society for Italic Handwriting
revised with the addition of original manuscripts
and printed books from the Bodleian Library

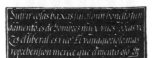 

EXEMPLAR SHEET: Society for Italic Handwriting.
The pens recommended for the italic hand are those
with a straight edge for right-handers and with a
left-oblique edge for left-handers. Either pen is held
so that it makes its thinnest line at an angle to the
writing-line of 45°: ∧ ∧ ⁄ ⁄ ⁄ ⁄
A simple alphabet: abcdefghijklmnopqrstuvwxyz.
A good practice is to copy the letters in this order: ilt
adgquceo bhkmnr vwy fs jp xz. The letters dfptx
are made with two strokes and e can be made with
one or two: e or c e. Alternative letters: ꝺ g ꝗ y ʒ ʒ.
Double letters: ff ff gg gg ss tt. By tracing this copy
with a dry pen one can learn the movements which
shape the letters. These drills may help: lll mmm uuu.
Much practice of a and n is desirable: aⲥⲥoa nrnn.

These letters have equal breadth of body: abdghnopqu.
Joins, both diagonal and horizontal, are necessary for
speed: nu un nun hum dim drum ai en den ever heed
fa fe fi fo fu ff fs ta te ti to tu ts tt oi oo os vow wavy.
Simple roman capitals without serifs go well with
italic letters: ABCDEFGHIJKLMNOPQRSTUV
WXYZ. These may be practised in groups: ILTHEF
OQCG AMNK DPBR I WY JUSXZ. A freer
alphabet of capitals is: ABCDEFGHIJKLMN
OPQRSTUVWXYZ. Capitals are not so high
as letters with ascenders: Gill John. Ascenders &
descenders (except for f t p) give double length: a d g.
Numerals may be as between 2 or 4 imaginary lines.
1234567890 1234567890 Stops: .:,;'s'""!?()&.
© Alfred Fairbank. 1960

At the Bodleian Library · Oxford
5 February – 31 March 1979 • Monday – Friday 9am – 5pm • Saturday 9am – 12.30pm

DESIGNED BY BERTHOLD WOLPE. PRINTED BY WESTERHAM PRESS

Posters, Periodicals and Occasional Printing

134

EXHIBITION POSTER

for an exhibition of Augustan Art at the Metropolitan Museum of Art, New York, 1938

The poster, set in 36 and 48pt Albertus Titling, was designed by Henry Watson Kent who used this type in other departments of the Metropolitan Museum as well.

Bruce Rogers, referring, in an address, to types without serifs, said: 'The latest (and a really admirable) version of this sort of letter, is one called "Albertus" ... recently used most effectively by Mr Kent in his posters and labels for The Cloisters'.* 54.5 × 39 cm

* The Work of Bruce Rogers: Jack of all trades, Master of one. New York, Oxford University Press, 1939

135

EXHIBITION POSTER

Wolperiana

Written with the broad pen in uncial and capital letters for an exhibition at the Studio am Mathildenplatz, Offenbach, October 1979

The title of the exhibition was taken from the Merrion Press book by E. M. Hatt and Charles Mozley (item 180). It consisted of work by members of the Wolpe family: Margaret L. Wolpe showed jewellery in silver; Sarah C. Lawrence (daughter) and Wolpe, graphic design; and Deborah H. Hopson (daughter), ceramics.

70 × 50 cm

136

EXHIBITION POSTER

Mexican Art Exhibition

Albertus used in a poster for an Arts Council exhibition held at the Tate Gallery, March to April 1953. It was designed and printed in black and red by the Shenval Press under the direction of James Shand. 76 × 50 cm

137

EXHIBITION POSTER

A Show of Hands

An exhibition arranged by the Society for Italic Handwriting in collaboration with the Bodleian Library. 1979

Designed by Berthold Wolpe. The masthead is printed in red with the lettering reversed out. The wording is set in Hyperion. The composition includes wood-blocks from 16th-century writing-masters and an italic exemplar by Alfred Fairbank. Printed at the Westerham Press. 39 × 25.5 cm

138

WORLD RADIO

First Radiolympia Number
London, British Broadcasting Co.
28 August 1936

a. Proof of cover with type (Corvinus) in black and border in red

b. Cover, as used, with type in red and border in blue

The border shows an early use of Wolpe's Fanfare Press typographic ornaments.

both 32 × 25 cm

139

THE SHOE HORN

London, Properts Ltd, 1939

Cover of a house magazine designed by Berthold Wolpe for the Fanfare Press.

25 × 18.5 cm

140

THE JOURNAL OF EDUCATION

Oxford University Press

Berthold Wolpe designed the cover for this journal in 1940 using Albertus Titling and a device of a tree.

a. Green cover with printing in red. July 1940

b. Special American Number. November 1941

For war economy reasons the title, etc., was reduced to a heading above the list of contents. It was printed in black on the text paper.

both 28.5 × 22 cm

141

ROYAL AIR FORCE JOURNAL

Proof of cover for issue of July 1942

Set in Tempest type with an RAF device designed by Berthold Wolpe, the cover design was prepared and first used in 1941.

25 × 18 cm

THE

142

MID-DAY

Proof of cover printed in red on green paper

Berthold Wolpe designed the cover for John Watney, the editor. The one and only number of this magazine was published in Oxford in the winter of 1946/7. Its cover was printed in black on red paper with an oval cut-out showing the names of the contributors.

24 × 15.5 cm

143
SIGNATURE
Original drawing for title-piece

Signature, a quadrimestrial of typography and graphic arts, was edited and published by Oliver Simon from 1935 to 1940. A new series was started in 1946 and it ran until 1954. This title-piece was used on the covers of the first three issues of the revised series.   4.2 × 28 cm

146
EAGLE and GIRL
Logos for Eagle and Girl magazines published by the Hulton Press. The editor was Marcus Morris and Ruari McLean the design adviser, who commissioned this work from Berthold Wolpe. The two designs were produced in 1950 and 1951 respectively.   25 × 19 cm

TIMES

144
THE TIMES MASTHEAD
When The Times decided to make changes in the make-up of the paper, Berthold Wolpe was asked to design a new masthead.
a. The Times: first use of the new design, 3 May 1966. Last used 20 September 1970.
b. Five proofs of The Times front page made to try out the different mastheads drawn by Wolpe. These trials were only for internal use.
c. Original drawing of one of the mastheads submitted by Wolpe.

147
EARLY MUSIC
Edited by John Thompson
Oxford University Press, October, 1979
Cover design and lettering by Berthold Wolpe.
24 × 18.5 cm

148
GREGYNOG PRESS
National Games League of Wales
Certificate of Merit
Newton, Gregynog Press, 1939
A diploma in Welsh for the Youth Eisteddfod which Berthold Wolpe designed for the Gregynog Press. A laurel border surrounds text set in Albertus and a coat of arms with a Welsh dragon. John Beedham engraved the arms and border on wood.   33.5 × 29 cm

145
TIMES LITERARY SUPPLEMENT
London, Times Newspapers Ltd
17 March 1972
Wolpe's front-page design incorporating uncial lettering for a special number: Irish Writing Today   42 × 30 cm

149

DINNER INVITATION
Double Crown Club

Berthold Wolpe's design for an invitation to the
fiftieth dinner on 9 October 1935 was printed at
the Fanfare Press. The Double Crown device
was used on the club notepaper for some years.

25 × 19 cm

150

INVITATION CARD
for an exhibition of contemporary furniture
by seven architects at Heal's Mansard Gallery,
1936
Drawn by Berthold Wolpe and printed at the
Fanfare Press. 14 × 11.3 cm

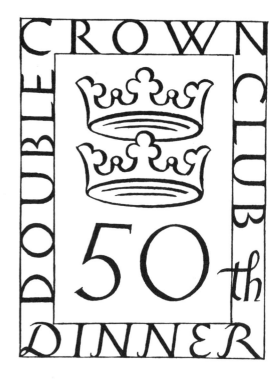

151

CHRISTMAS CARD
Proof, on Japanese paper, of a line block, shar-
pened with the burin. The designer's own
Christmas card for 1937. 10.5 × 10 cm

152

NEW YEAR'S CARD
The initials of the designer and those of his wife,
as well as the connecting ampersand, are drawn
in one continuous line. 1941/42 13 × 20 cm

153

WESTERHAM PRESS

Christmas card for 1953

Set in Hyperion with drawings by Berthold Wolpe who made these originally for GOOD FOOD FROM ABROAD by Salome Andronikov, published by Harvill Press the same year.

20.5 × 11 cm

154

CHRISTMAS CARD FOR R.B.F.

Richard Bertram Fishenden, editor of the PENROSE ANNUAL, was a great authority on the technique of printing. For many years he commissioned a different artist to design a Christmas card, which had always to incorporate a fish. c.1950   25 × 19.5 cm

155

FOLDER FOR TRAVEL TICKETS

Designed for Killick Martin Ltd and printed by the Westerham Press. c.1950   22 × 13.5 cm

156

MENU

25th Anniversary Dinner of the Faculty of Royal Designers for Industry

Three pages set in Hyperion type, and printed in black and red, in grey paper cover, at the Westerham Press, 1962. Berthold Wolpe also contributed the RDI jubilee device for the cover. The format is slim and of pocket size, unlike many outsize menus produced for similar occasions.   30 × 15 cm

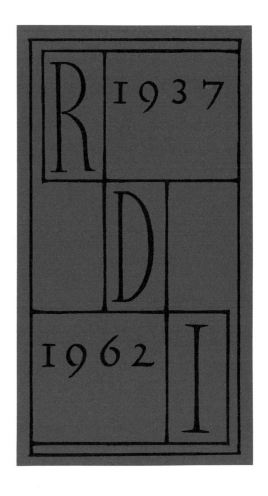

The Faculty of Royal Designers for Industry

RENAISSANCE
HANDWRITING

An Anthology of Italic Scripts

by

Alfred Fairbank

and

Berthold Wolpe

FABER AND FABER LIMITED

24 Russell Square

London

The Designer as Author and Editor

157

BERTHOLD WOLPE
Schriftvorlagen für Schreiber, Buchdrucker,
Maler, Bildhauer, Goldschmiede, Stickerinnen
und andere Handwerker
Herausgegeben von Rudolf Koch
Kassel-Wilhelmshöhe, Bärenreiter-Verlag
[1934]
A collection of samples of lettering for the use of
calligraphers, printers, painters, sculptors, goldsmiths, embroiderers and other craftsmen.
Descriptive page of contents and fourteen plates
showing alphabets and some of their applications. First edition in orange cover. Second
printing [1949] in green cover.   21 × 30 cm

158

RUDOLF KOCH
and Berthold Wolpe
Das ABC-Büchlein
Zeichnungen von R.K. und B.W.
in Holz- und Metallschnitten von Fritz Kredel
und Gustav Eichenauer
Leipzig, Insel-Verlag, 1934
This book is not a copy-book in the usual sense
but a collection of more or less spontaneous
alphabetical compositions and it was done, as
Koch said 'for the fun of it.' Some of the
alphabets are lighthearted, while some follow
stricter styles but all show a certain spirit of
enjoyment.   15 × 23 cm

159

RUDOLF KOCH
and Berthold Wolpe
The little ABC book of Rudolf Koch
with a memoir by Fritz Kredel
and a preface by Warren Chappell
London, Merrion Press, 1976

This book, which includes a facsimile of the original ABC-Büchlein, was printed in the USA at the Meriden Gravure Company, in 2500 copies (1000 of them for David R. Godine, 300 for the Merrion Press, 650 for the friends of the Klingspor Museum and 550 for The Typophiles as Chap Book Fifty-Three).

In a four-page leaflet which accompanied this work, Wolpe said: 'after so many years ... I am struck by their freshness and exuberance. I am sure Rudolf Koch, whom we used to call the Master, would have been happy that this particular enterprise is the one we have chosen for celebratory publication in 1976'.   15 × 23 cm

160

BERTHOLD WOLPE
Handwerkerzeichen
Frankfurt am Main, Bauersche Giesserei, 1936

Thirty-five signs of crafts and trades designed for the Bauer Type Foundry. The preliminaries and captions are set in Hyperion type, which was originally called Matthias Claudius. This was the first showing of the type.

The captions are set in both German and English. The former show the use of Fraktur capitals. Though they are successful in this book, their use was discontinued.   18 × 12 cm

161

BERTHOLD WOLPE
Schmuckstücke und Marken
Frankfurt am Main, Bauersche Giesserei, 1938

The forty-five devices in this book, some cut on wood and some on metal, were designed between 1925 and 1937. The collection contains book plates, colophons, trade marks, seals, cover and book decorations, etc. The Bauer Type Foundry printed 150 copies on handmade paper water-marked b g. The book was designed by Wolpe and it shows an early use of his Hyperion type.   23.5 × 17.5 cm

162

BERTHOLD WOLPE, editor
A Newe Booke of Copies 1574
A facsimile of a unique Elizabethan Writing
Book in the Bodleian Library, Oxford
London, Lion and Unicorn Press,
Royal College of Art, 1959

This edition was limited to 200 copies. A trade
edition was published by the Oxford University
Press in 1962. It reproduces one of the earliest
printed writing-manuals to be published in England.   25 × 22 cm

163

ALFRED FAIRBANK
and Berthold Wolpe
Renaissance Handwriting
an Anthology of Italic Scripts
London, Faber & Faber, 1960

Designed by Wolpe, set in Van Dijck and Fell
types and printed at the University Press,
Oxford.
This book, which contains 108 plates, anno-
tated in detail by Wolpe and a substantial introduction by Alfred Fairbank, is a standard work
of reference for students of the history of handwriting and the modern italic hand.
                                                                29 × 23 cm

164

BERTHOLD WOLPE
Caslon Architectural
on the origin and design of the large letters
cut and cast by William Caslon II
James Moran Ltd, for the Kynoch Press, 1964

Fifty copies bound in cloth were reprinted for
the author from Alphabet 1964. The first
monograph on these little-known printing
types.   28.5 × 22 cm

165

BERTHOLD WOLPE
Florilegium Alphabeticum
Alphabets in Medieval Manuscripts'
in CALLIGRAPHY AND PALAEOGRAPHY:
Essays presented to Alfred Fairbank.
Edited by A. S. Osley
London, Faber & Faber, 1965

This essay was Wolpe's contribution to a
festschrift for Alfred Fairbank on his 70th
birthday. Typography by Wolpe. Printed at the
University Press, Cambridge.   25 × 19 cm

166

BERTHOLD WOLPE
Vincent Figgins Type Specimens, 1801 & 1815
with an introduction and notes
London, Printing Historical Society, 1967

Wolpe accompanied this facsimile of his own
unique copies of Vincent Figgins' type specimens with an extensive introduction. Review-
ing the book, Nicolas Barker wrote: 'there is
considerable food here to sustain a substantially
revised picture of early 19th-century type-
founding.' It was printed by the John Roberts
Press in Clerkenwell.   24 × 16 cm

167

STANLEY MORISON
and Esther Potter
Splendour of Ornament
Preface by Berthold Wolpe
London, Lion and Unicorn Press, 1968

The designer of this colourful book was
Graham Percy, a student in the School of
Graphic Design at the Royal College of Art. As
Wolpe was the tutor who supervised this ven-
ture, he was asked by Robin Darwin to provide a
preface.

This book gives an account of the writing master G. A. Tagliente's book of embroidery ornaments, the first printed work of its kind to be published in Italy.

No.325 of an edition of 400 copies

26.5 × 22.5 cm

168

BERTHOLD WOLPE, editor
Freedom of the Press
London, Printing Historical Society, 1969

The four broadsheets shown here, from the second and third decade of the nineteenth century, were selected for their content and visual appeal from English and French specimens in the editor's possession. On each of these, the actual printing machines of the period, the Stanhope, the Columbian and the Albion presses or their French equivalents are shown. Two English and two French broadsheets were printed in facsimile by Rotaprint Limited and a fifth sheet, with notes by Wolpe, by Eyre & Spottiswoode.

51 × 35.5 cm

169

BERTHOLD WOLPE, editor
Johann David Steingruber
Architectural Alphabet, 1773
With an introduction and some account of Steingruber's life and work by Berthold Wolpe, RDI
London, The Merrion Press 1972

Thirty-three plates are reproduced in facsimile and twenty-four illustrations appear in the text which is set in Monotype Van Dijck and Oxford Fell Type. Printed at the University Press, Oxford by Vivian Ridler, to the design of Montague Shaw.

Each of the plates shows an imposing building constructed on a ground plan formed by the outline of a capital letter of the roman alphabet.

35.5 × 26 cm

170

BERTHOLD WOLPE
John de Beauchesne and
the First English Writing Books

Preliminary notes from a study of the work and life of John de Beauchesne. Fifty copies in paper covers were reprinted in 1975 from an article in the Journal of the Society for Italic Handwriting. 22.5 × 16 cm

171

BERTHOLD WOLPE, editor
Characters Well Marshalled
Gutenberg's Portrait in North's Plutarch
(1657)
with a Description of Letter-cutting, Casting and Printing from Thevet's Pourtraitures
of 1579
Introduction by Berthold Wolpe
with a translation by A. S. Osley
Wormley, The Glade Press 1977

From the colophon: 'An edition of 27 copies printed by hand and bound by Dr A. S. Osley at the Glade Press, Wormley in Spring 1977. The misprint on page 5 (1567 for 1657) was an ignoble victory of the subconscious over the super-ego. LAUS DEO'. 20 × 13 cm

JOHN GUTTEMBERG
a Moguntian, the Inventor
of the Art of Printing

172

A. S. OSLEY
and Berthold Wolpe
Scribes and Sources
Handbook of the Chancery Hand in the
Sixteenth Century
London, Faber & Faber, 1980

The book was designed by Berthold Wolpe, set in Ehrhardt and printed by B A S Printers Ltd, Over Wallop, Hampshire.

From the preface: 'Dr Berthold Wolpe has kindly contributed the chapter on Beauchesne. He has been carrying out research into the life and work of this writing-master for some years and plans to publish a book on him in due course'. 25 × 18 cm

2 Whitehall Court S.W.1   24 March 1960

My Dear Wolpe: You and Fairbank are most
kind to have presented me with a copy of your
handsome volume on Renaissance Handwriting,
a truly exciting contribution to the subject.   I offer
my heartiest congratulations to you and your great
collaborator on the writing (I mean of the text)
and the production (I mean the printing) of the work.

The book arrived on Wednesday and I write on
Thursday.   I have had time only to turn over the pages
but I see at a glance what a feast of good things the
authors have here provided.   The Introduction and the
Plates, not the mention the Description are notable.   The
whole forms a splendid; if I am right about the existing
literature on the subject, unique presentation of the
script in all its beauty.

I am also grateful to you for a copy of the so-limited
edition of your reproduction of the Newe Booke of Copies
1574 of whose existence, I need not say, I was unaware.
This is a fine piece of editing .   The mere sight of the excellent
facsimiles gives me great pleasure.

Do, please, convey my felicitations to Fairbank . Excuse
the bad writing of this letter .   My sight is not what it
used to be.

Again, all grateful thanks and congratulations
Yours
Stanley Morison

Miscellanea

173

MARTIN LUTHER

Der kleine Katechismus für Haus, Schule und Kirche
Offenbach am Main, Buchdruckwerkstatt der Technischen Lehranstalten, 1929
Rudolf Koch inscribed this book to Berthold Wolpe, his 'collaborator and friend' ('Zum Anfang seiner Lehrtätigkeit seinem Mitarbeiter und Freund') when Wolpe began his work as a teacher. Koch's signature is dated 24 October 1929. Wolpe records: 'I was a student with Rudolf Koch and later became his assistant . . . I owe him more than I can say.' (Print in Britain, Vol. 1, No. 2, June 1953.)   14.5 × 10.5 cm

174

EXHIBITION POSTER

Rudolf Koch und sein Kreis
Poster designed by Rudolf Koch for an exhibition of his work and that of his circle. The exhibition was held at the Frankfurter Kunstverein in January 1932. The central panel shows the personal marks of the eight participants, seven of which are variations of the orb and cross mark, which was the general sign of the workshop. Fritz Kredel and Berthold Wolpe were, at that time, Koch's principal assistants at the Offenbach art school. The two bottom lines are set in Koch's Neuland type.   61 × 47 cm

175

LETTER OF THANKS
To London from Offenbach
December 1932

In this light-hearted and colourful letter to Alex Gumb illustrated with block-proofs and drawings, Rudolf Koch, Berthold Wolpe, Fritz Kredel and Richard Bender express their thanks for the gift of a dart board.

See plate H   30.5×43 cm

176

EXHIBITION POSTER
Die neue Sammlung
Munich, April/May [1933]

Poster designed by Berthold Wolpe for an exhibition of the Offenbacher Werkstatt: Rudolf Koch, Fritz Kredel, Karl Vollmer, B.W. and others. The poster was written with a broad pen and then cut on linoleum.   84.5×59.2 cm

177

TWO TRIBUTES
a. Testimonial from Rudolf Koch
dated 22 February 1934

Berthold Wolpe has been for some years my best co-worker in the field of lettering. He combines this with excellent personal qualities and I would like to speak for him, as because of his personal modesty, his interests are not represented by anybody and his excellent work does not find nearly the appreciation in public, which it deserves.

Certified copy   30×21 cm

b. Letter from the Reichskammer der Bildenden Kunst, Berlin
dated 28 February 1935

'… as you are Non-Aryan and as such do not possess the necessary reliability to create and spread German cultural values, I forbid you to further practise your profession as a graphic designer.'   19×21 cm

178

NICOLETE GRAY
'Berthold Wolpe'

Her illustrated article on the work of Berthold Wolpe appeared on pp. 20–27 of Signature, No.15, December 1940.   25×18.5 cm

179

RICHARD GUYATT
A drawing of Berthold Wolpe with accompanying text

One of six portraits which appeared in Motif 5, edited by Ruari McLean and published in London by Shenval Press, 1960.   31×24.5 cm

180

CHARLES MOZLEY
Wolperiana
An illustrated guide to Berthold Wolpe
With various observations by Charles Mozley
Introduction by E. M. Hatt
London, Merrion Press, 1960

Printed on the hand-press by Susan Mahon in a limited edition of 335 numbered copies. Nos. 1–150 are signed. The text set in 10, 12 and 16pt Hyperion. Photograph by Frank Herrmann.

20×12 cm

181
MORISON LETTERS
Six autograph letters from Stanley Morison to Berthold Wolpe

a. 14 January 1937
Refers to the hound designed by Wolpe for the Albertus specimens and mentions a design which he has put in hand for setting using 'the new &'. 25.5 × 20 cm

b. 8 September 1939
Morison confirms that 'the drawings [type designs] have arrived safely'; mentioned that he has had a letter from C. E. Poeschel (dated 31.8.'39): 'We understand each other perfectly...'. This letter was published by Wolpe in his obituary of Morison in the Journal of the Society for Italic Handwriting, No.53, Winter 1967. 25 × 19 cm

c. 3 January 1940
Morison regrets being unable to keep a lunch appointment ... wants to speak to Wolpe about Albertus Light, of which he enclosed a specimen. 25 × 20 cm

d. 12 March 1940
Morison refers to Wolpe's layout for the Gutenberg memorial piece in Signature, No.14, May 1940, and states that he has been promised a proof of Albertus Light for 14 March.
25 × 20 cm

e. 24 March 1960
Thanking Wolpe for the gifts of RENAISSANCE HANDWRITING and the NEWE BOOKE OF COPIES. 33 × 20 cm

f. 28 December 1965
Thanking Wolpe for the present of 'the great Fairbank Festschrift ... a major contribution to knowledge and understanding of the script we use.... Osley's volume is a notable addition to the literature ... To you, my dear Wolpe, I am indebted for a fascinating article from which I learned much.'

In a footnote to his signature: 'With apologies for this accelerated cursive.' 27 × 23 cm

182
SMALL POSTER
for Stanley Morison Memorial Lecture
Morison and others: Reminiscences of a type designer
An illustrated lecture by Berthold Wolpe RDI

This poster, of unusual format, was produced by the Faculty of Art and Design, Manchester Polytechnic, where the lecture was given on 26 January 1977. The type used is Albertus. Colours: yellow and two tones of brown.
30 × 34 cm

183
BEATRICE WARDE
Typography in Art Education
The Association of Art Institutions and The National Society for Art Education. 1946
The frontispiece is set in Albertus and has as its text a shortened version of Beatrice Warde's 'This is a printing office'. Inscribed by the author: BW from BW March 5 '47 18 × 12 cm

BIBLIOGRAPHY

Books and articles by Berthold Wolpe

Das ABC Büchlein, with Rudolf Koch, Insel-Verlag, Leipzig, 1934; Merrion Press, 1976

Schriftvorlagen, Bärenreiter-Verlag, Kassel [1934] and [1949]

Handwerkerzeichen, Bauer Type Foundry, Frankfurt am Main, 1936

Schmuckstücke und Marken, Bauer Type Foundry, Frankfurt am Main, 1938

A Book of Fanfare Ornaments, Fanfare Press, 1939

'Notes on the selection of type for the printing of books' in Printing Review, No.53, Summer 1950

'The fore-runners of the picture press' in The Times Printing Supplement, July 1955

'A note on simple binding' in The Calligrapher's Handbook, ed. by C. M. Lamb, 1958

'Pepys's copy of Moxon's Mechanick Exercises', with Harry Carter, in The Library, Vol.14, No.2, June 1959

'Rudolf Koch, der Meister' in Philobiblon, Vol.3, No.3, 1959

Renaissance Handwriting, with Alfred Fairbank, Faber, 1960

'A royal manuscript by Arrighi Vicentino in the British Museum' in The Book Collector, 1960

A newe book of copies 1574 (ed.), Lion and Unicorn Press, 1959; Oxford University Press, 1961

'Caslon Architectural' in Alphabet, 1964

'Florilegium Alphabeticum: alphabets in medieval manuscripts' in Calligraphy and Palaeography, Faber, 1965; in Philobiblon, Jahrgang ix.4, December 1965

Vincent Figgins Type Specimens 1801 and 1815, Printing Historical Society, 1967

'Stanley Morison' in The Journal of the Society for Italic Handwriting, No.53, Winter 1967

'Two versions of a sonnet in Raphael's hand' in The Journal of the Society for Italic Handwriting, No.54, Spring 1968

Splendour of ornament (on) the first Italian manual of decoration, Venice, 1524, by Giovanni Antonio Tagliente. Stanley Morison and Esther Potter, preface by B. Wolpe, Lion and Unicorn Press, 1968

Freedom of the Press, Printing Historical Society, 1969

'The Printing Historical Society' in The Penrose Annual, Vol.62, 1969

Architectural alphabet 1773 (facsimile of J. B. Steingruber's alphabet), Merrion Press, 1972; George Braziller, New York, 1975

'Harry Carter: a view of early typography up to about 1600' in The Library, March 1974

'John de Beauchesne and the First English Writing Books' in The Journal of the Society for Italic Handwriting, No.82, Spring 1975; also published in Scribes and Sources by A. S. Osley, Faber, 1980

'Fairbank at 80' in The Journal of the Society for Italic Handwriting, No.83, Summer 1975

'Sir Francis Meynell' in The Journal of the Society for Italic Handwriting, No.84, Autumn 1975

'The Bookman', a seventy-fifth birthday celebration for Richard Herbert Ingpen de la Mare, June 1976 (unpublished)

'A tribute to Jan Tschichold from London', Jan Tschichold (Kunstgewerbe Museum), Zürich, 1976

'A quartet of italics' in The Journal of the Society for Italic Handwriting, No.96, Autumn 1978

General

'Rituelle Kunst' by G. Haupt, Soncino Blätter, Berlin, c.1929

'Arbeiten von Berthold Wolpe' by G. Haupt in Frankfurter Israelitisches Gemeindeblatt, Frankfurt am Main, April 1930

'A new titling' (anon.) in Signature, No.3, 1936

'Book jacket design' by G. Brown in The Penrose Annual, Vol.38, 1936

Rudolf Koch der Schreiber by G. Haupt, Leipzig, 1936

'The Double Crown Club' by F. Sidgwick in Signature, No.2, 1936

'Necessities and novelties' by R. Harling in The Penrose Annual, Vol.39, 1937

'Black letter: its origins and current use' by S. Morison in The Monotype Recorder, Vol.36, No.1, 1937

'The work of Berthold Wolpe' by N. Drew in Art and Industry, Vol.28, No.167, 1940

'Berthold Wolpe' by N. Gray in Signature, No.15, 1940

The Art of the Book Jacket by C. Rosner, London, 1949

'Type for display' by A. Davis in British and Colonial Printer, March 1953

'Victorian revival' by R. Harling in The Penrose Annual, Vol.41, 1953

Lettering of today by E. Hölscher et al., London, 1954

'Berthold Wolpe, type designer' (anon.) in The New Mechanick Exercises ed. by E. Howe, part X, 1957

'Choice of Types' by K. Day in Print in Britain, Vol.5, No.8, 1957

Modern Book Design by R. McLean, London, 1958

'Berthold Wolpe' by R. Guyatt in Motif, No.5, 1960

Wolperiana by C. Mozley, London, 1960

The Twentieth-century Book by J. Lewis, London 1967

Tradition und Erneuerung (anon.), ed. by E. Stein, Frankfurt am Main, 1972

'Berthold Wolpe', a mid-twentieth-century typographical interlude (anon.) ed. by W. A. Shepherd, Plymouth, 1973

'Wolpe, book designer' [by J. Moran] in Printing World supplement: Book design and production, 1974

The Double Crown Club: a history of fifty years by J. Moran, London, 1974

Rudolf Koch: a report on the exhibition held at the Klingspor Museum, Offenbach am Main, by R. Beyer, November 1976 (unpublished)

'B.L.W. at 70' by A. S. Osley in The Journal of the Society for Italic Handwriting, No.87, 1976

Berthold Wolpe: a survey of his work by S. E. M. Fowler (degree thesis), Reading, 1977 (unpublished)

The Cornford Oration by C. Cornford, RCA, London, 1979

INDEX